A NEW YORK TIMES COMPANY PUBLICATION NYT

Family Circle
LOW-COST MAIN DISHES

EDITOR: NANCY A. HECHT
ART DIRECTOR: MARSHA J. CAMERA
ART ASSOCIATE: WALTER SCHWARTZ
PRODUCTION MANAGER: NORMAN ELLERS

Cover photograph by George Nordhausen

Food tested in Family Circle's Test Kitchen by Dora Jonassen, Home Economist

CONTENTS

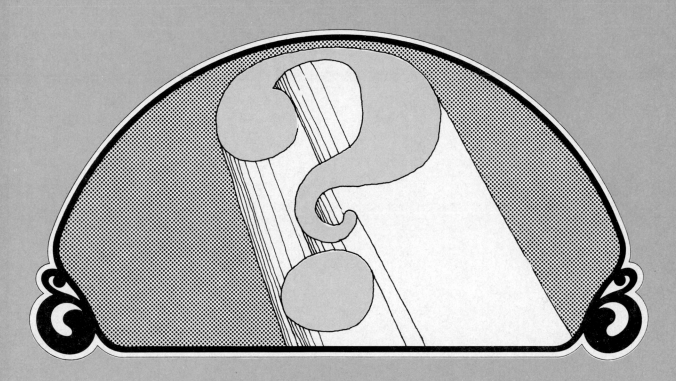

1
EATING BETTER, SPENDING LESS

We all know what's happened to food prices. They've increased. There are many reasons for this, including the fact that our demand for more food has grown tremendously. But reasons can't solve the one problem we face every day: "How can I balance the budget and still feed my family the foods they love?" This book is dedicated to answering the question—practically, imaginatively and always with an eye on good, sound nutrition. This first chapter can start you off on the right foot, with dozens of tips on saving in the supermarket and at home. Our recipe chapters also include valuable ideas on buying, storing and preparing various basic foods, plus hundreds of recipes geared to the low budget. All prove that you can eat well in spite of inflation, and that what happens to your menus is more often a matter of good planning than money.

EATING BETTER, SPENDING LESS

What follows is a series of ideas to help you keep the family food budget in line. The tips are practical, easy-to-learn and realistic for even the most hurried shopper. For even further ideas, see the Eating Better, Spending Less pages included in the recipe chapters.

• Plan your menus a week at a time and, if possible, shop only once a week. By planning ahead you can plan for leftovers *and* make use of what you already have on hand.

• Check your newspaper and grocery store ads for weekly specials and sales. They'll help you plan your menus according to the best buys. But don't buy sale items your family won't eat— you'll simply be wasting money. Incidentally, newspapers and magazines often offer discount coupons that can save you a great deal over a year's time. Keep the coupons you'll really use; give friends those you won't.

• Make a shopping list, grouping items by the order you find them in your store. Once in the market, stick to your list, but if you find a better buy, be flexible.

• Plan at least ⅓ of your weekly menu around advertised meat specials.

• Become familiar with brand names so you can recognize price changes. A price increase in one brand might tell you to compare brands and perhaps switch to a lower-priced brand. On the other hand, an increase may indicate an increase in quality. Read the labels carefully to find the best buy nutritionally and cost-wise.

• Compare costs for the same food in the fresh, frozen and canned sections of your supermarket. Which is the best buy? To find out, divide the price by the number of servings. The lower price per serving is your best buy. . . whether it's fresh, frozen or canned.

• For another comparison of values, buy by weight rather than volume, package size or number. For instance, buy fresh produce by the pound and compare weights of loaves of bread, not sizes.

• Eat before you shop. If you go to the store hungry, your shopping list doesn't stand a chance.

• Never economize on nutrition. Shop for foods that are good sources of the important nutrients and buy as many of these as your budget allows, in the greatest possible variety.

• Base weekly menu planning on the Basic Four nutritional groups. For quick reference, here is a breakdown of the basic four:

FOOD GROUP	SERVINGS PER DAY
Meat (Or chicken, fish, dried beans, eggs & liver)	Two 4-ounce servings (boneless portions)
Milk	Four cups for teenagers and under; two cups for adults
Fruits (one citrus) and Vegetables (dark green or dark yellow)	2 servings of each
Bread and Cereals	2 servings of each

NOTE: The next time you shop, list the foods you buy opposite the group they belong in. If you occasionally check your buying this way, you'll be sure your family is getting a well-balanced menu.

• Buy according to storage space. Family-size bags of frozen foods are economical but not if they spoil because of improper storage.

• How much will your family eat? The large, economy-size may be a good buy but for a twosome the small-size may prove more worthwhile. The reason? It will give you menu variety and eliminate leftovers. When leftovers do accumulate, keep them in the front of the refrigerator where they're more likely to be eaten than forgotten.

• When you shop only once a week, avoid waste by using perishables first. Canned and frozen foods can carry you through the latter part of the week.

• If your family likes milk, buy it in half-gallon or gallon containers, rather than in quarts. And for cooking and baking, use instant nonfat dry milk in the largest container you can use up within a reasonable time; or use evaporated milk mixed with water. For drinking, you might try nonfat dry milk on your family. If they don't care for it, try mixing it half and half with fresh milk. Cup for cup nonfat dry milk supplies the same important nutrients as whole milk—at a big saving.

• Day-old baked breads, rolls and cakes are usually marked down but are as fresh as if you'd bought them yesterday and stored them at home. If you have enough freezer space, buy enough of these marked down baked goods for a week at a time. Also, storing bread in the refrigerator or freezer extends the freshness and can drastically cut down on the amount you end up throwing away because of staleness or mold.

• Save the tag ends of breads and those that are too dry for ordinary use. Crushed, grated, cubed and toasted they make great toppings for casseroles, coatings for chops or croutons for soups and salads.

• Use leftovers wisely. Small quantities of left-over vegetables can be used in soups or combined with other vegetables as a new side dish.

• Store foods properly. When you return home from the grocery store—and after meals—put food away quickly to avoid spoilage and waste. This is especially important for perishable items.

• Shop competitively, perhaps at two or three supermarkets, to take advantage of the sales in each. (Of course, this is only really practical if the stores are reasonably close together.)

UNIT PRICING

• If your store has a unit-pricing system, take advantage of it. This system informs consumers how much a product costs per pint, quart or pound. If you don't have unit pricing, here's how to figure the cost of an item per unit measure: Convert pounds to ounces for a total number of ounces. For example, one pound, seven ounces equals 23 ounces. Then divide the cost by the number of ounces and you'll get the unit cost. If more than one item is offered for a fixed price, i.e., three cans for 89¢, you can figure the unit price by multiplying the number of cans by the ounces in each can. Then divide the cost by the total ounces for all three cans.

• Unit pricing is a good budget-watcher, but remember it is not a guide to quality. In order to accurately figure your best buys, check the unit prices on items of the same quality—not of two different qualities. Also, it pays to occasionally buy two different brands of the same weight and compare the actual quantity of food in each. Water or syrup can sometimes make up a large portion of the weight in one can, while in

another can you may get more solids.

OTHER POINTS TO REMEMBER

• When buying items like popcorn, rice, macaroni, spaghetti and so on, always check to see which size package is the best buy in terms of cost-per-pound and enriched product. Obviously a two-pound package at 59¢ is a far better bargain than a pound for 38¢. You can also save money by passing up "frills" such as preflavored popcorn and built-in popping pans. Also, if you buy the popcorn salt-and-butter flavoring to add to melted margarine you'll spend about 10 times less—and it looks and tastes great.

• Imitation sour cream is less expensive than the real sour cream. When used in hot dishes like stroganoff and lasagna, you can't tell the difference from the real thing. Dips made from imitation sour cream are just as tasty—and about half the price for twice the amount!

• All chain supermarkets have their own brands. Buying these products instead of name brands almost always results in savings. A general range of products to be found under supermarket brands are canned and frozen vegetables and fruits, sandwich spreads, oils and shortenings, paper products, tea and coffee, soft drinks, laundry products. In other words, almost everything! Store-brand margarine, for example, is lower in price than shortening. Store-brand flour has no coupons or recipes, but it's enriched and lower in price than others.

• Plan for snacks. Homemade snacks such as cookies, fruit drinks and milk-based drinks are usually less expensive than store-bought snacks, and are often more nutritious.

• Remember, non food items are not part of your food bill. You might buy laundry items, cosmetics, etc., in your supermarket, but you should list these items separately on your monthly household budget.

• Buy staples such as flour, sugar and cornmeal only once or twice a month, if possible. Most grocery products cost less per serving when you buy larger sizes.

• Check sales of two, three, four or five items for one price. They usually mean big savings if the foods are ones your family likes.

• Cheese prices vary with choices to suit all needs. Generally, the highest priced ones are the aged natural cheeses; the lowest in price, the process varieties, particularly in large packages. All are rich in protein.

• Large cuts of meat on special mean a bargain in price per pound—as well as meat for several meals. (See meat tips, page 11, and on pages 14 and 17 in Chapter 2.)

• Think of bacon as a flavor extra as well as a meat choice. A few slices diced, cooked and stirred into scrambled eggs stretch a little a long way. The drippings make ideal seasoners for vegetables and salads, too.

• Experiment with spices and seasonings. Most of the great flavor-makers—garlic, mustard, Worcestershire sauce, chili, catsup, horseradish —are relatively low in cost and quick to use. Using a wide range of seasonings and flavor enhancers adds variety at minimal cost, encourages consumption of fruits and vegetables, increases the use of foods that are low in calories and reduces the need for sauces that are too costly.

• When buying foods for lunchboxes, compare the cost of presliced and packaged cold cuts to those sold in a solid piece. Often you pay a higher price for the convenience of slicing and special packaging. Cheeses, too, vary greatly in price, depending on whether the cheese is sliced and sold in individually wrapped slices.

• Make oven heat do double or triple duty. Bake a stew along with a roast, or a big squash in the shell to peel, cut up and glaze invitingly for another meal, or cook your whole meal in the oven at one time. By using your oven for double-duty cooking, you'll be helping to cut down on your gas or electric bill.

• Depend on hearty macaroni, noodles and dried beans to see you through a meatless meal or one with only a little leftover meat.

• If you have a large family or a freezer, it pays to buy broiler-fryers packed two, three or more in a plastic bag. The birds are cleaned and ready to roast, or you can cut them up and use in all kinds of main dish casseroles, soups and salads.

• Be flexible with your shopping list. Jot down "alternatives" in case one food is a better buy than another. For example, a special on canned peaches may mean savings over the fresh ones you originally planned on. Also, remember to carry menu insurance—a standby meal for days when time-saving is all-important. The choices here can range from complete frozen dinners to canned and frozen main dishes and vegetables, all ready to heat-and-serve. You may pay a little

more for the convenience, but the time saving may very well be worth it.

• Bulk oatmeal is one place for large savings. The round cartons of oatmeal cost twice as much per pound as the five- or nine-pound packages which are available in both the old-fashioned and the quick-cooking varieties. If these large packages seem like a lot to use up, consider the many ways you can use oatmeal—in cookies, meat loaves, as toppings for casseroles, etc. Also, the difference between the instant and quick-cooking varieties of cereal is only about five minutes in time, but a lot of money per pound!

• Another way to save on cereal purchases is to buy those that are unsweetened or without dried fruits. You can add your own sugar and fresh fruits for much less money.

BUYING CONVENIENCE FOODS

• Select a minimum of built-in convenience. You'll be surprised at the number of products that can be bought at lower prices if you are willing to do the peeling, slicing or mixing.

• Make selections from the frozen foods section last and put them in your freezer as soon as you return home. Frozen foods stay in prime condition longer if they're not subject to drastic temperature changes, and if your freezer is set at 0° and below. If the freezer section of your refrigerator doesn't have its own temperature gauge, it may be a good idea to invest in an an inexpensive refrigerator/freezer thermometer. They're usually sold in supermarkets or in the housewares section of department stores.

• Frozen potatoes are often cheaper than fresh ones and they offer a time-saving too. They can be fried or boiled for use in a potato salad.

• Instant nonfat dry milk can also be whipped if mixed with equal parts of lukewarm water or fruit juice. When soft peaks are formed, add 2 tablespoons of lemon juice for each ½ cup dry milk. Add sugar and flavorings only after stiff peaks form. Use instead of cream; you'll save!

• Avoid pre-mixed spice combinations. They're costly. For example, a three-ounce bottle of cinnamon and sugar sells for many times more than to mix this combination yourself. Also, avoid herbs and spices in fancy bottles. Instead, buy plain containers or boxes and transfer the spices to your own decorative bottles at home. You're paying extra for packaging!

Right: The raw ingredients for a hearty, meal-in-one bean dish that offers the ideal way to stretch a small amount of meat. On page 10, you'll see the oven-baked results. See chapter 6 for bean recipes.

• Use bouillon cubes or envelopes of instant broth in lieu of canned broth which costs more.
• Bake your own cakes instead of buying prepared ones or mixes. It's about 75 percent cheaper.
• Make your own pancake batter from scratch instead of from a mix or ready-to-pour package.

FRUITS & VEGETABLES

• If you select fresh fruits and vegetables that are not pre-packaged, don't pay extra for perfectly round, red apples, round onions or splotchless grapefruits and oranges. There's no difference in taste or nutrition—only in price. Also, medium-size fruits and vegetables are generally less expensive than large ones.
• Save the liquid from cooked or canned fruits and vegetables. Store in refrigerator and use for soups, stews, casseroles, for meat cooking or in lieu of water in gelatin desserts.
• Use all vegetable scraps for soup stock. Don't throw anything away.
NOTE: Turn to page 108 for additional tips on buying and cooking fruits and vegetables.

YOUR MEAT DOLLAR

Chapter 2 includes dozens of ideas for trimming the fat off your meat dollar. But here are a few general ideas to keep in mind:
• When you buy meats, use the cost per serving not the cost per pound, as your main guide to value. For example, a boneless pot roast may cost more per pound than a bone-in pot roast. But because there's no bone, you'll get more servings out of the boneless roast and spend less for each of those servings. To remember this rule, use the following as a guideline: One pound of boneless meat is enough for four servings; one pound of meat with a bone will give you two servings; and one pound of really bony meat will provide just one serving.
• Look for unadvertised specials in the meat case. Oftentimes, meat is repriced lower when it gets a bit older. There's no loss of nutrients—in fact, aging helps tenderize meat.
• Supplement meat with other protein foods. A smaller portion of meat served with pasta, bread, cheese, milk, eggs, yogurt, cottage cheese or cooked vegetables will provide enough nu-

trients to meet the daily requirements of each member of your family. The following list of foods in the quantities given supply the same amount of protein as one ounce of meat:

  3 **slices of bread**
1 ½ **cups cooked rice**
1 ½ **cups cooked oatmeal**
  1 **cup cooked pasta**
  ½ **cup all-purpose flour**
  2 **tablespoons peanut butter**
  1 **egg**
  ¼ **cup cashews, walnuts, almonds**
  ¼ **cup pumpkin, sesame or sunflower seeds**
  3 **tablespoons creamed cottage cheese**
  1 **ounce of cheese**
  ⅔ **cup milk**
  ¾ **cup yogurt**
  ⅓ - ½ **cup cooked beans or peas**

• Use trimmed fat from meat for browning instead of shortening. Two tablespoons of melted fat are enough to brown a four-pound roast.
• Stretch your meat dollar with ready-to-serve canned meats. On a cost-per-serving basis, chopped beef, luncheon meat and chopped ham represent good buys. The reasons? Since each variety of canned meat is made from carefully trimmed beef or pork and is completely cooked in the canning process, there is no shrinkage in home preparation. One 12-ounce can will make a satisfying main dish for four people. Canned meats offer storage convenience, too.
• Prepackaged meat items offer another advantage—every package has a label which fully describes the product. The USDA requires that each label carry the product name, a list of ingredients, the net weight, the name and address of the manufacturer or distributor and the legend and the number of the federally inspected plant. The product name such as "ham", "bacon" or "bologna" appears prominently in bold type. Some products contain an extender such as nonfat dry milk, cereal or soy protein. Each of these wholesome, less-costly ingredients must be specifically identified in a prominent manner, with a statement such as Nonfat Dry Milk Added. Usually, these meat items offer an inexpensive substitute for other meats.
• Cook all meat at low temperatures (300°-325°). Meats cooked at low temperatures shrink less, are more tender and have more flavor than those cooked at high temperatures.

2
DOLLAR-SAVING MEAT DISHES

There are no two ways about it—Americans love meat. So much so that most of us include this basic food in at least one meal a day. However, cost fluctuations and shortages can sometimes daunt the staunchest meat fan. But there's no real reason to be discouraged when you realize that with planning and some knowledge of the meat department in your supermarket, you can trim the fat off your meat bill and still satisfy family appetites. For example, there are ways, as outlined on pages 18 and 19, to turn one roast into three separate, freshly-cooked meals. There are other ways to stretch a tiny bit of meat a long way, as demonstrated in our casserole, pasta and soup chapters. Further, on the next 17 pages you'll find a good selection of recipes and ideas for using budget cuts of meat in ways that will please the most discerning palate.

MEAT: EATING BETTER, SPENDING LESS

GENERAL MEAT TIPS

• Use every bit of meat you buy. Melt down fat trimmings for drippings, and simmer bones and lean cuttings for soup stock or gravy. Time-saver tip: Shop for a week's supply of meat at once, trim it all before storing, then take care of the trimmings in one swoop.

• In general, it isn't thrifty to buy on sales to stock your freezer. Why? Supermarkets routinely feature the same cuts, and there's no need to tie up meat money in freezer inventory. A better plan: Buy extra cuts that appeal to you on any shopping trip and freeze them to use when needed. Veal, for example, isn't always available, but when it is, that's the time to buy enough for several meals and freeze it.

• Buy meat in terms of meals; leftovers that are not enough for a second meal are expensive.

• Meat sales are one of the first steps to economy. The United States Department of Agriculture reports that the more expensive the cut, the less often it is featured. But when it does go on sale, the price drop is greater. For example, porterhouse steak may be advertised once in five weeks, but the price is then cut about 30¢ a pound. As a weekend special, even popular ground beef may be 10¢ a pound cheaper than usual.

• Always buy well-trimmed meat with an even fat covering and lean flecked with fat—that's all you need for flavor. Remember that meat at $1.29 a pound costs 8¢ an ounce, and any excess fat you trim away costs the same amount.

• Save on meat by buying larger cuts and slicing your own steaks and chops. For example, one large loin of pork will give you enough meat for a pork roast, pork chops and barbecued backbones (see illustration on page 18).

• But don't become your own butcher unless you have to. Check the price of the cut-up meat. Sometimes it's the same price per pound as the big piece you would have to cut up yourself.

• Remember that grades in meat indicate appearance only. The highest grade "U.S. Prime" (sold mainly to restaurants) has no more food value than the lowest grade, "Standard." "Choice," the second grade, is the grade available in most supermarkets. Choose the grade that offers you the best price.

• Chill canned meats such as chopped ham, beef, pork luncheon meat or corned beef before you slice them. They'll cut more neatly and in thinner, more uniform slices, giving you more servings for your money.

• If shopping for one meal, never buy more meat than you need. When you repeatedly throw away little bits of leftovers, you are throwing away real money. Approximately 63¢ goes into the garbage when you discard 1 cup (5 ounces) of leftover meat that costs 99¢ a pound as purchased. Such meat could be slivered and reheated with crisp-cooked mixed vegetables. Serve on rice and you have a Chinese dinner.

• Invest in a sharp little boning knife and a good-quality carving knife. Keep them razor-sharp. If you want to cut a bargain roast into steaks, you're all set.

• Buy a wooden (or metal) meat mallet. This is the original "tenderizer," and a must when you want to turn slices into thin cutlets.

BEEF

• Generally, beef is in the greatest supply and at the lowest prices from mid-winter to spring; lamb and pork, from mid-winter to late spring; veal from late spring to mid-summer. It may, therefore, pay to stock up on meat during this time (particularly during February, March and April).

• Watch for savings on large packages of ground beef. Those weighing more than five pounds often cost 3¢ to 5¢ a pound less than smaller sizes. If you have a freezer, make up several meat loaves and freeze part. Or shape a supply of patties and freeze for sandwiches.

• Don't get hung up on ground beef. Ground lamb or veal patties are usually priced about the same as ground beef and give menus a new lift.

• For steak on a budget, choose chuck, bottom round or shoulder steak. Marinate or tenderize the meat first, then broil or grill to medium-rare for maximum tenderness.

• Chuck roast on sale? Buy a thick one; then, at home, cut it into pieces for a Swiss-steak dinner. Savings will be 20¢ to 30¢ a pound over the store-cut meat tagged SWISS STEAK.

• When porterhouse and T-bone steaks are the same price, pick porterhouse—it has a larger tenderloin.

• Flank steak, sometimes marked LONDON BROIL, is usually not an economical cut. One reason is supply; (please turn to page 17)

there are only two on each animal. For your money, the tender broiling steaks—porterhouse, T-bone, sirloin or top round—offer more enjoyable eating.

• Which is thriftier—a thick family-size steak or thinner individual steaks for each serving? Surprising as it may seem, the family-size one. For example, a three-pound boneless sirloin cut 1¼ inches thick will make six servings. You'll need at least five pounds of T-bone steaks to serve six. Individual steaks would only be a value, if you were planning a meal for one or two.

• Attractively priced alternates for a rib roast: Sirloin tip or rump roast. Prime or choice grades may be oven-roasted and have little waste.

• The smaller muscle of a blade-bone chuck steak can be broiled if you use tenderizer on it. Cook to desired doneness and top with buttery crumbs that have been tossed with grated lemon and orange rind. The larger muscle can be pot-roasted in a sauce flavored with leftover wine or beer. Both meals serve 4 if you start with a 3-pound steak.

• A small eye of round roast goes a long way if you make it into sukiyaki. Freeze the meat until barely firm, then cut into paper-thin slices and pound with a meat mallet. Stir-fry slices in a bit of oil; add fresh spinach, slivered celery and onions, and soy-flavored beef broth. Cook briefly. Serve with rice.

• You can feed all the party guests lavishly with teriyaki hors d'oeuvres made from one 1½- to 2-pound flank steak. It's solid meat, but needs to be tenderized by scoring with a knife on both sides. Freeze until just firm, then cut on the diagonal into very thin slices. Thread accordion-fashion on a skewer; marinate in a pungent baste; broil; serve hot.

• If beef shank is really a bargain, buy it to cube for stew or braise whole for individual roasts.

• Nutritionally, liver packs a wallop. Slice thin, and broil to rare. Or, put through the food chopper and add to meat loaf. The price is right.

• Ever try beef heart? The flavor is excellent. Cut out the fat, veins and arteries; wash thoroughly. Cut into strips. Braise with onions and herbs until fork tender.

• Rediscover canned corned beef, beef stew, chopped beef, meat in barbecue sauce. For a couple, or a small family, the cost per serving is sometimes cheaper than starting from scratch, because there is no waste.

• Beef-shank crosscuts, at least 1½ inches thick, make perfect individual pot roasts at penny-pinching prices.

• Most meat counters carry ready-cubed beef for stewing. But because store labor and meat trimmings cost money, you'll rate a double dividend if you buy beef chuck and cut it up yourself, then simmer the bone and trimmings for broth for soup.

• All kidneys—beef, pork, lamb and veal—are good buys, with no waste. Prices remain fairly steady, and because all kinds work equally well in recipes, you can depend on what's available.

VEAL AND LAMB

• Veal and lamb for stewing often cost less than the same cut of beef, and if your market is having a sale, you'll find these stew meats a delectable way to stretch your budget.

• For keeping your budget and yourself fit, lamb breast really measures up.

PORK & HAM

• When you want fresh pork, compare the price of pork shoulder with a leg cut (fresh ham). The shoulder may cost so much less that you can add on an extra pound or two of meat for the same total price.

• Fresh pork hocks are a bargain when your budget's in a squeeze, even though it takes a pound for each serving.

• Consider all ham prices and buy what fits your purse and purpose. Whole or half smoked hams are usually the same price per pound. And though a butt portion may be a few cents higher per pound than a shank end, it's a better choice because you get more meat. Center steaks are the most expensive.

• Count on pork sausage for dinner as well as for breakfast—it makes an easy hearty meal. Your best buy: Bulk sausage. Because of fixing time and labor, patties are priced about 10¢ higher; links, about 20¢ higher.

• Fancy-quality bacon may not be your most frugal buy. Use the regular sliced kinds for showy platters, but for sandwiches or recipe ingredients, ends and pieces, cuts or slab bacon net big flavor at substantial savings.

Left: Boeuf Sauté Bordelaise treats ground beef to red wine and mushrooms. It's a convenient skillet dinner you can make in minutes. The recipe is included in this chapter.

HOW TO GET THREE MEALS FROM A PORK LOIN ROAST

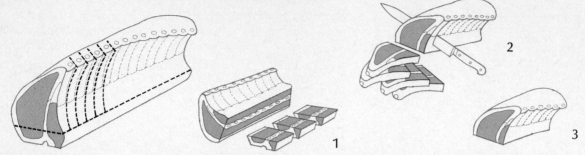

Start by selecting a good-size rib cut of pork loin. (1) Have the butcher saw through the ribs, high enough to leave an inch-thick layer of meat on the backbones. Have him chop the backbones into serving-size pieces. Cook as you would spareribs. (2) Cut chops for another meal from the remaining roast by slicing between the ribs. (3) Cook the remaining piece of meat as a pork roast for your third fresh-cooked dinner.

HOW TO MAKE FOUR MEALS FROM HALF A HAM

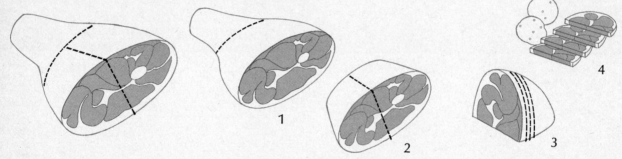

Choose a full-cut shank half of ham. (1) Have the butcher saw off a generous end for making a "boiled" dinner with carrots, onions, potatoes and cabbage. (2) Divide the center part of the ham into two portions. Bake the piece with the bone. (3) Cut the large end of the boneless piece into thick slices for frying or broiling. (4) Cut the smaller end into thin slices for use in making a dish of scalloped ham and potatoes.

HOW TO MAKE THREE MEALS FROM ONE PORK BUTT

For three economy meals, buy a five- to seven-pound fresh pork shoulder. (1) Cut as shown to divide into two pieces. Use the piece with the bone for a one-meal roast. (2) Cut steaks from the large end of the bone-less piece, about a half-inch thick. Braise the steaks as you would pork chops. (3) Cut the small end of the boneless piece into half-inch cubes. Use the diced pork for chop suey or a casserole of corn and pork.

HOW TO MAKE TWO MEALS FROM A RIB ROAST

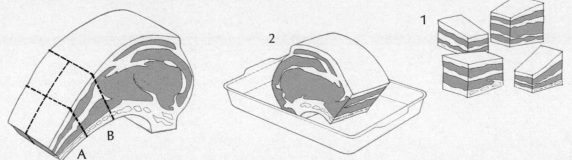

While not an economy cut in itself, beef rib roast can be budget-minded if you plan two meals from one roast. Have your butcher saw through the bones at A and B. (1) Then cut between the ribs to make individual servings of short ribs. (2) Now, for your roast, you have the tenderest "heart" of the piece you bought. To get more servings—and to make it juicier—keep oven heat at 325° to cut shrinkage to a minimum.

HOW TO GET THREE MEALS FROM ONE POT ROAST

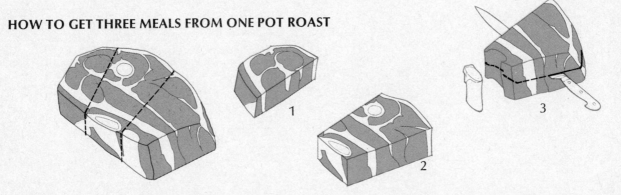

With a simple bit of cutting in your kichen, you can get three meals from a thick round-bone pot roast like the one above. (1) From the round end of the roast, cut a piece to use in a beef-and-vegetable stew. Cut this boneless piece into cubes. (2) Then from the center, cut a thick piece for a chunky pot roast. (3) With a sharp knife and a saucer under your hand for safety, split the remaining piece for two Swiss steaks.

HOW TO GET THREE MEALS FROM ONE LEG OF LAMB

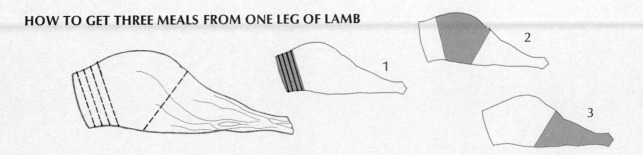

Buy a full-cut leg of lamb. Ask your butcher to cut off a few lamb steaks and to cut through the shank, leaving about a pound of meat on the bone. (1) Broil the lamb steaks as you would loin chops. (2) Use the easy-to-carve center portion of the leg for a roast. (3) Later, cut the meat from the shank into cubes for another freshly cooked meal. Use these tender, boneless pieces in an Irish stew, lamb curry or shish kebab.

BURGUNDY BEEF LOAF

    1 cup Burgundy
    ¼ cup finely chopped celery
    1 clove garlic
    1 bay leaf
    2½ pounds ground round or chuck
    2½ cups soft bread crumbs (5 slices)
    1 large onion, finely chopped (1 cup)
    1 tablespoon chopped parsley
    2 teaspoons salt
    ¼ teaspoon leaf rosemary, crumbled
    ¼ teaspoon leaf thyme, crumbled
    ¼ teaspoon pepper
    2 eggs
    1 can condensed beef broth
    1 teaspoon Worcestershire sauce
    ¼ cup water
      Burgundy Sauce (recipe follows)

1. Combine wine, celery, garlic and bay leaf in a small saucepan; bring to boiling; lower heat; simmer, uncovered, until volume is reduced to half, about 10 minutes. Remove and discard garlic and bay leaf; cool wine mixture completely.
2. Combine beef, bread crumbs, onion, parsley, salt, rosemary, thyme and pepper in a large bowl; add the wine mixture, eggs, ½ cup of the beef broth (reserve remaining broth for sauce) and Worcestershire. Mix until well-blended. Shape into an oval loaf on a lightly oiled shallow baking pan.
3. Bake in moderate oven (350°) 1 hour and 10 minutes, until loaf is a rich brown. Remove with 2 wide spatulas to a heated serving platter; keep warm. Add reserved broth and ¼ cup water to drippings in the pan; bring to boiling, stirring constantly to loosen browned bits. Strain into a 1-cup measure. (Add water, to make 1 cup.)
4. Make Burgundy Sauce.
5. Arrange small buttered whole carrots, onions and sauteed mushrooms on platter with loaf, if you wish; sprinkle with chopped parsley. Serve with Burgundy Sauce. Makes 8 to 10 servings.

BURGUNDY SAUCE—Sauté 1 tablespoon chopped shallots or green onion in 2 tablespoons butter or margarine in a medium-size saucepan about 5 minutes; stir in 3 tablespoons flour; gradually add the reserved broth and ½ cup Burgundy. Cook, stirring constantly, until sauce thickens and bubbles 3 minutes. Stir in 1 teaspoon chopped parsley. Makes about 1½ cups.

VEGETABLE-BEEF LOAF

    2 tablespoons butter or margarine
    1 small zucchini squash, shredded (1 cup)
    1 small onion, chopped (¼ cup)
    1 can (1 pound) Italian tomatoes
    2 pounds meat-loaf mixture
    1 cup soft bread crumbs (2 slices)
    2 eggs
    ½ cup milk
    2 teaspoons salt
    ¼ teaspoon pepper
    ¼ teaspoon leaf marjoram, crumbled
    ¼ teaspoon leaf thyme, crumbled
Sauce:
    2 tablespoons chopped onion
    1 envelope or teaspoon instant beef broth
    ½ cup boiling water
    ¼ teaspoon salt
    ⅛ teaspoon pepper

1. Melt butter or margarine in skillet; sauté zucchini and onion until tender. Chop 2 of the canned tomatoes; add to zucchini mixture. Cool the entire mixture slightly.
2. Combine zucchini mixture, meat-loaf mixture, bread crumbs, eggs, milk, salt, pepper, marjoram and thyme in a large mixing bowl. Mix until well-blended. Pack mixture into a lightly oiled 9x5x3-inch loaf pan; turn out into baking pan.
3. Bake in moderate oven (350°) 1 hour and 10 minutes. Remove to serving platter; keep warm.
4. Make sauce: Sauté onion in pan drippings in baking pan. Dissolve beef broth in boiling water. Chop remaining tomatoes; add with beef broth to onion. Cook, stirring constantly, until sauce thickens, about 3 minutes. Add salt and pepper. Spoon over meat loaf. Garnish with sliced, stuffed olives, if you wish. Makes 8 servings.

CHOUCROUTE GARNI

    2 cans (1 pound, 11 ounces each) sauerkraut
    6 ham hocks, weighing about 3 pounds
    2 cups dry white wine
    1 bay leaf
    6 whole cloves
    1 medium-size onion, peeled
    1½ pounds knockwurst
    1 red apple, quartered, cored and sliced
    12 new potatoes (about 1¼ pounds)
(Please turn to page 23 for directions.)

Right: Choucroute Garni (garnished sauerkraut) combines ham hocks and knockwurst with a delicious blend of seasonings, sauerkraut and potatoes. Recipe is in this chapter.

1. Soak sauerkraut 5 minutes in cold water in a large bowl; drain well.

2. Place ham hocks in a Dutch oven or a large heat-proof casserole. Add drained sauerkraut, wine and bay leaf. Press cloves into onion; press onion down into sauerkraut. Heat to boiling; reduce heat; cover. Simmer very slowly 1½ hours, tossing with a fork once or twice, or until ham hocks are almost tender.

3. Score knockwurst with a sharp knife; place on sauerkraut; simmer 20 minutes longer. Add apple slices, pushing them down into sauerkraut; cook 10 minutes longer.

4. Scrub potatoes well; cook in boiling salted water to cover in a medium-size saucepan 20 minutes, or until done.

5. Arrange choucroute with potatoes on a large deep platter. Serve with wholewheat bread and individual servings of mustard, if you wish. Makes 6 servings.

BEER-BRAISED LOIN OF PORK

  1 **pork loin roast, about 5 pounds**
  3 **large onions, chopped (3 cups)**
  1 **pound carrots, peeled and diced**
  1 **bottle or can (12 ounces) dark beer**
  2 **teaspoons salt**
  ¼ **teapsoon pepper**
  1 **bay leaf**
  5 **whole cloves**

1. Brown pork loin well on all sides in a kettle or Dutch oven; remove from pan. (Or brown in a large heavy roasting pan on surface burners.)

2. Sauté onions and carrots until soft in pork drippings. Stir in beer, salt, pepper, bay leaf and whole cloves. Return pork to kettle and cover. (If using roasting pan, cover tightly with aluminum foil.)

3. Braise in moderate oven (350°) 2 hours, or until pork is tender when pierced with a two-tined fork. Place pork on platter and keep warm.

4. Pour cooking liquid from kettle into a large bowl. Skim off fat; remove bay leaf. Place liquid and solids in container of electric blender and whirl at low speed until smooth (or press through sieve). Pour sauce into saucepan. Heat to boiling, stirring often. Stir in a little gravy coloring, if you wish. Generously spoon the sauce over the pork after it has been sliced. Makes 8 servings.

DOUBLE PEPPER BEEF

  2 **medium-size green peppers, halved, seeded and thinly sliced**
  2 **medium-size sweet red peppers, halved, seeded and thinly sliced**
  2 **tablespoons olive oil or vegetable oil**
  1 **chuck steak fillet (about 1½ pounds)**
  1 **cup water**
  1 **teaspoon Italian seasoning, crumbled**
  1 **teaspoon salt**
  ¼ **teaspoon pepper**

1. Sauté peppers in oil until soft in large skillet; remove to hot platter; keep warm.

2. Cook steak in oil remaining in skillet, turning once, 5 minutes on each side or until steak is as done as you like it. Slice steak and arrange with peppers on hot platter.

3. Stir water, Italian seasoning, salt and pepper into skillet. Cook, stirring constantly, scraping to loosen cooked-on juices in skillet. Boil 3 minutes to reduce volume by one-third. Pour over sliced beef and peppers. Serve with hot cooked rice, if you wish. Makes 6 servings.

SUKIYAKI

  1 **chuck steak fillet (about 1½ pounds)**
  ¼ **cup vegetable oil**
  2 **medium-size sweet potatoes, pared and thinly sliced**
  ½ **pound green beans, tipped and cut in 1-inch pieces**
  1 **small green pepper, halved, seeded and cut into thin strips**
  1 **small sweet red pepper, halved, seeded and cut into thin strips**
  1 **cup thinly sliced celery**
  ½ **cup soy sauce**
  1 **cup water**
  1 **small head Chinese cabbage, shredded**
  1 **bunch green onions, trimmed and cut into 2-inch pieces**
  4 **large mushrooms, trimmed and sliced**

1. Trim all fat from steak; cut meat into very thin strips. (For easier cutting of raw beef, partially freeze steak 1 hour to firm meat.)

2. Heat oil in a large skillet with a cover. Add steak strips and sauté, stirring occasionally, 2 to 3 minutes, or until brown; remove with a slotted

Left: Beer-braised Loin of Pork. The pork is browned, then baked in beer along with onions, carrots and seasonings.

spoon and keep strips warm. Reserve for Step 5.
3. Add potatoes, green beans, green and red pepper, and celery; sauté 2 to 3 minutes, or until vegetables start to soften.
4. Combine soy sauce and water in a cup; pour over vegetables; cover. Simmer 5 minutes. Stir in shredded cabbage, green onions and mushrooms; cover. Cook 5 minutes longer, or until cabbage wilts and vegetables are crisply tender.
5. Return cooked steak strips to pan and heat until piping-hot. Serve with hot cooked rice and more soy sauce, if you wish. Makes 6 servings.

KÖNIGSBERG MEATBALLS

      4 slices bread
    ½ cup milk
      2 pounds meat-loaf mixture
      1 can (2 ounces) anchovy fillets, drained and chopped
      3 eggs
      1 small onion, grated
      2 tablespoons grated lemon rind
      1 teaspoon salt
    ¼ teaspoon pepper
      2 envelopes instant beef broth or 1 teaspoon granulated beef bouillon
      4 cups water
    ¼ cup (½ stick) butter or margarine
    ¼ cup flour
      1 teaspoon sugar
    ½ cup dry white wine
      2 tablespoons well-drained capers
      1 tablespoon lemon juice

1. Place bread slices in single layer in a shallow dish; pour milk over; let stand until absorbed (about 10 minutes); break apart with fork into small pieces.
2. Combine meat-loaf mixture, half the anchovies, eggs, onion, lemon rind, salt, pepper and bread in a large bowl, mixing lightly. Shape into 32 balls.
3. Combine beef broth and water in a large skillet; heat to boiling; add meatballs, lowering into boiling broth with a slotted spoon. Simmer, uncovered, 15 minutes, or until no longer pink in center (break one open to test). Remove with slotted spoon to a deep platter. Reserve cooking liquid.
4. Make sauce: Melt butter or margarine in a medium-size saucepan; stir in flour and sugar;

cook until bubbly, stirring constantly. Gradually add wine and 2 cups of the cooking liquid, continuing to stir until mixture is thickened and bubbles 1 minute. Stir in capers, lemon juice and remaining half of anchovies, stirring until anchovies are blended into sauce. Spoon over meatballs. Serve with a side portion of sauerkraut and mashed or boiled potatoes, if you wish. Makes 8 servings.

PARSLIED STEAKS

      6 frozen chopped beef steaks (from a 2-pound package)
      4 tablespoons butter or margarine
      4 green onions, trimmed and chopped
    ½ cup chopped parsley
    ½ teaspoon salt
    ½ teaspoon leaf marjoram, crumbled
    ¼ teaspoon cracked or coarse grind pepper

1. Sauté steaks on both sides, following label directions, in butter or margarine in a large skillet; remove to hot platter, overlapping steaks; keep warm while making sauce.
2. Sauté green onions in drippings in skillet until soft; stir in parsley, salt, marjoram and pepper; heat just until bubbling. Pour down center of steaks. Frame with broccoli spears and pan-browned or mashed potatoes, if you wish. Makes 6 servings.

DEVILED CHUCK BROIL

      1 bone-in chuck steak (about 2 pounds)
    ⅔ cup wine vinegar
      2 tablespoons vegetable oil
      1 small onion, chopped (¼ cup)
      2 tablespoons prepared mustard
    ½ teaspoon cracked or coarse grind pepper
      2 cups soft white bread crumbs (4 slices)
      2 tablespoons melted butter or margarine

1. Trim any excess fat from steak and score remaining fat edge every inch. (Reserve a few pieces of fat.) Place steak in a shallow dish.
2. Mix vinegar, oil, onion, mustard and pepper in a bowl; pour over steak. Marinate in refrigerator, turning once, at least 2 hours.
3. Remove steak from marinade and pat dry

with paper toweling.

4. Rub broiler rack with a few fat trimmings to prevent sticking. Broil steak 4 inches from heat, 5 minutes; turn steak; broil 5 minutes longer, or until it is as done as you like it.

5. While steak broils, toss bread crumbs with melted butter or margarine in a small bowl.

6. Remove broiler pan from heat; top steak evenly with prepared crumbs. Return steak to broiler and broil 2 minutes longer, or until crumbs are golden. Remove to serving platter; slice and serve. Makes 6 servings.

LAMB RIBLET STEW

    4 pounds lamb riblets or breast of lamb, cut into serving-size pieces
    ½ pound medium-size onions, peeled and quartered
    2 cups water
    3 teaspoons salt
    1 teaspoon Worcestershire sauce
    ½ teaspoon leaf rosemary, crumbled
    ¼ teaspoon pepper
    6 medium-size potatoes, pared and cut into 1-inch pieces (about 2 pounds)
    1 large sweet potato, pared and cut into 1-inch pieces (about 10 ounces)
    1 leek, washed and sliced ¼ inch thick
    1 tablespoon butter or margarine
    ¼ cup flour
    ⅓ cup water

1. Heat a kettle or Dutch oven over medium heat. Brown lamb, a few pieces at a time, removing pieces as they brown. (No need to add extra fat for browning.) Saute onions in drippings in kettle 10 minutes, or until nicely browned. Remove; reserve.

2. Return meat to kettle; add water, salt, Worcestershire, rosemary and pepper. Heat to boiling; lower heat; cover; simmer 30 minutes. Add potatoes, sweet potatoes and onions, pushing them down under liquid. Simmer 40 minutes longer, or until meat and potatoes are tender. Meanwhile saute leek in butter or margarine in small skillet, 10 minutes, or just until tender. (Do not brown.)

3. Lift out meat and vegetables and arrange on a shallow heated serving dish along with leek; cover and keep warm.

4. Let fat rise to top of meat-vegetable broth;

skim off all possible fat; heat broth to boiling.

5. Blend flour and water in a small cup; stir into boiling broth. Cook and stir until gravy thickens and bubbles 1 minute. Pour over lamb. Sprinkle with chopped parsley, if you wish. Makes 6 servings.

MAKE-EASY LAMB STEW

    3 pounds lean shoulder of lamb, cubed
    2 teaspoons salt
    2 bay leaves
    4 cups water
    1 can (1 pound) whole onions, drained
    1 can (1 pound) whole potatoes, drained
    1 can (1 pound) lima beans, drained
    4 tablespoons flour
    ⅓ cup cold water
    3 tablespoons chopped parsley

1. Combine lamb, salt, bay leaves and water in a kettle or Dutch oven. Heat to boiling; reduce heat; cover; simmer 1 hour, or until meat almost falls off bones.

2. Lift out meat with a slotted spoon; let cool until easy to handle, then take meat from bones and trim off fat.

3. Let fat rise to top of broth and skim off; remove bay leaves. Return lamb to broth; add onions, potatoes, lima beans; cover; heat 15 minutes.

4. Blend flour and water in a small cup; stir into stew. Cook and stir until gravy thickens and bubbles 1 minute. Serve in soup plates or shallow bowls. Sprinkle with chopped parsley. Makes 8 servings.

OVEN-GRILLED CHEDDAR STEAK

    1 chuck beef steak, weighing about 3½ pounds
      Instant unseasoned meat tenderizer
    3 tablespoons bottled steak sauce
    ¼ cup chopped pecans
    ½ cup grated Cheddar cheese

1. Remove steak from refrigerator 1 hour before cooking. When ready to cook, sprinkle with meat tenderizer, following the label directions; brush both sides with steak sauce; place on rack

in broiler pan placed close to the heat source.
2. Bake in very hot oven (450°) 25 minutes for rare, or until done as you like steak; remove from oven; turn off heat.
3. Sprinkle pecans, then cheese over steak; return to heated oven just until cheese melts.
4. Carve into ¼-inch-thick slices; spoon juices over. Makes 6 servings.

BRAISED LAMB WITH MARJORAM GRAVY

    1 boned lamb shoulder, rolled and tied (about 3 pounds)
    2 tablespoons vegetable oil
    ½ cup water
    1 medium-size onion, quartered
 1 ½ teaspoons salt
    ½ teaspoon celery seed
    ⅛ teaspoon pepper
    3 large potatoes, pared and cut into 2-inch cubes
    3 large carrots, pared and cut into thin strips
    3 large stalks of celery, cut into thin strips
    1 tablespoon flour
    ¼ teaspoon leaf marjoram, crumbled
    2 anchovy fillets, chopped

1. Brown meat on all sides in vegetable oil in a kettle or Dutch oven. Add water, onion, salt, celery seed and pepper; heat to boiling; lower heat; cover. Simmer 45 minutes.
2. Add potatoes and carrots, pushing them down into the broth; simmer 30 minutes. Stir in celery; simmer 30 minutes longer, or until the meat is tender.
3. Place lamb on a carving board; keep warm. Remove vegetables from kettle with a slotted spoon to a heated serving platter; keep warm while making gravy.
4. To prepare Marjoram Gravy: Pour cooking liquid into a 2-cup measure; let stand until fat rises to top. Skim off all fat; return 2 tablespoons fat to kettle. Add water to liquid to measure 1 cup.
5. Blend flour into fat in kettle; heat, stirring constantly, just until bubbly. Stir in the 1 cup liquid, marjoram and anchovies; cook, stirring constantly, until the gravy thickens and bubbles for about 1 minute.
6. Carve meat and place slices on platter with vegetables; spoon the Marjoram Gravy over the meat. Makes 6 servings.

BEEF GOULASH BUDAPEST

    1 bone-in chuck roast (about 3 pounds)
    4 tablespoons (½ stick) butter or margarine
    2 large onions, chopped (2 cups)
    1 small clove of garlic, crushed
    1 tablespoon paprika
    2 teaspoons salt
    ½ teaspoon caraway seeds
    4 ripe medium-size tomatoes, peeled and chopped
    ½ cup dry red wine
    3 tablespoons flour
      Water
      Cooked noodles

1. Trim bone and fat from beef; cut beef into 1-inch cubes; brown, part at a time, in butter or margarine in a kettle or Dutch oven; remove beef cubes as they brown; reserve.
2. Sauté onions and garlic in drippings in kettle until soft. Stir in paprika, salt and caraway seeds; cook 1 minute. Stir in tomatoes, wine and reserved beef cubes. Heat to boiling; reduce heat; cover. Simmer 1 hour and 15 minutes, or until beef is tender.
3. Blend flour with a little water in a cup to make a smooth paste; stir into bubbling goulash; cook, stirring constantly, until mixture thickens and bubbles 1 minute. Serve with cooked noodles. Makes 8 servings.

BRAISED STUFFED BREAST OF VEAL

    1 boned breast of veal (about 2¼ pounds)
    ¾ teaspoon salt
    ⅛ teaspoon pepper
    2 tablespoons chopped parsley
    ½ teaspoon leaf basil, crumbled
    ½ pound sausage meat (from a 1 pound package)
    1 cup grated carrots (about 3 large carrots)
    1 tablespoon butter or margarine
    ½ cup sliced celery
    1 medium-size onion, sliced
    1 can (about 14 ounces) chicken broth
      Water
    3 tablespoons flour

1. Spread breast of veal flat on a cutting board. (It should measure about 8"x15".) Please turn to page 29 for remainder of recipe.

Right: Oven-grilled Cheddar Steak, a bargain-best steak choice topped with cheese and chopped pecans. Recipe is in this chapter.

Sprinkle with salt, pepper, parsley and basil. Combine sausage meat with grated carrots in a small bowl; spread evenly over surface of veal, pressing firmly. Roll up veal from short end, jelly-roll fashion. Tie crosswise with heavy string at 1½-inch intervals.

2. Brown meat in butter or margarine in Dutch oven; add celery and onion; sauté 5 minutes longer. Add chicken broth; simmer, covered, 2 hours, or until meat is tender. Remove meat to a carving board.

3. Strain pan juices through a sieve; press vegetables through; pour into a 2-cup measure; add water if necessary to make 1¾ cups. Return to Dutch oven.

4. Combine flour and 6 tablespoons water in a 1-cup measure; blend until smooth. Pour into juices in Dutch oven. Cook, stirring constantly, until sauce thickens and bubbles 3 minutes.

5. Remove string from veal; cut into thin slices; serve with vegetable sauce. Makes 8 servings.

DUCHESS SAUTÉED BEEF LIVER

- 1 egg yolk
- 2 cups mashed potatoes (about 4 medium-size potatoes)
- ¼ cup flour
- 1½ teaspoons salt
- ¼ teaspoon pepper
- 1½ pounds sliced beef liver
- 2 tablespoons vegetable oil
- 2 medium onions, sliced
- 1 green pepper, cut lengthwise into strips
- 1 tomato, cut into wedges
- 1½ cups water
- 1 envelope or teaspoon instant beef broth

1. Beat egg yolk into mashed potatoes; spoon into pastry bag fitted with a star tip. Pipe potatoes in a border around edge of a 10-inch, round ovenproof platter or board.

2. Bake in hot oven (400°) 15 minutes, or until potatoes are golden-brown.

3. Meanwhile mix flour, salt and pepper on wax paper. Cut liver into serving-size pieces, if needed; coat with flour mixture.

4. Sauté liver in hot oil in a large skillet 4 minutes on each side, or until brown and done as you like liver. Arrange slices, overlapping, inside border of potatoes. Keep hot at lowest oven temperature.

5. Saute onions and pepper strips in same skillet, adding more oil if needed, 10 minutes, or until soft and golden. Stir in tomato; sauté 2 minutes longer. Arrange on top of liver.

6. Add water and instant beef broth to skillet. Bring to boiling, stirring and scraping to dissolve browned bits. Simmer, uncovered, 2 minutes. Pour over liver. Sprinkle with chopped parsley, if you wish. Serve at once. Makes 6 servings.

SPICY GLAZED HAM

- 1 fully cooked bone-in ham, weighing about 10 pounds
- 1 cup dark corn syrup
- ⅔ cup firmly packed brown sugar
- 2 tablespoons prepared mustard

1. Place ham, fat side up, on a rack in a shallow roasting pan. Insert meat thermometer into the thickest part of meat without touching bone.

2. Bake in slow oven (325°) 2¼ hours; remove from oven; cut away the rind and score the fat.

3. Mix corn syrup, brown sugar and mustard in a small bowl; brush part over ham.

4. Continue baking, brushing several times with glaze, 30 minutes, or until richly glazed and thermometer registers 140°

5. Remove to a heated serving platter. Let stand 20 minutes before slicing. Makes 16 servings.

HAM AND SAUSAGE LOAF

- 1 cup corn bread stuffing mix (from an 8-ounce package)
- ¼ cup boiling water
- 1 can (8 ounces) cream-style corn
- 1 egg
- ½ cup chopped parsley
- 1 pound cooked ham, ground (4 cups)
- 1 pound bulk sausage
- ¼ cup dark corn syrup

1. Combine corn bread stuffing mix with boiling water in a large bowl. Blend in corn, egg and parsley. Add ham and sausage; mix lightly until well-blended.

2. Moisten a 6-cup melon mold or bowl and pack meat mixture firmly into mold; invert loaf onto shallow baking pan. (Turn to page 30.)

Left: Braised Stuffed Breast of Veal, a main dish that proves low-cost cooking can be entirely gourmet. Recipe is in this chapter.

3. Bake in moderate oven (350°) 1 hour and 15 minutes. Brush loaf with syrup and bake 15 minutes longer, or until loaf is well-glazed. Serve on platter garnished with glazed sweet potato slices and buttered asparagus, if you wish. Makes 6 servings.

VEAL MARENGO

- 1 package (8 ounces) medium egg noodles
- 1 tablespoon butter or margarine
- 1 tablespoon vegetable oil
- 6 frozen breaded veal patties (about 1½ pounds)
- 1 can (1 pound) whole boiled onions, drained
- 1 can (4 ounces) whole mushrooms, drained
- 1 envelope (1½ ounces) spaghetti sauce mix
- 1 can (1 pound) tomatoes
- 1 can (1 pound) tomato wedges
- ½ cup garlic croutons
- 2 tablespoons chopped parsley

1. Cook noodles following label directions; drain. Spread in shallow 8-cup baking dish.
2. Heat butter or margarine with oil in large skillet; sauté veal patties about 3 minutes on each side. Overlap browned patties down center of noodles. Keep warm.
3. Toss onions and mushrooms in same skillet to brown lightly. Arrange around patties.
4. Add spaghetti sauce mix to same skillet with tomatoes and juice from the can of tomato wedges. Stir over low heat until sauce bubbles.
5. Tuck the tomato wedges around the veal patties. Pour the sauce over all. Sprinkle with croutons.
6. Bake in a hot oven (400°) 20 minutes, or until sauce is bubbly. Sprinkle with chopped parsley. Makes 6 servings.

SCANDINAVIAN PORK POT

- 1 rib-end pork loin, about 7 ribs, backbone cracked (about 3 pounds)
- 2 tablespoons vegetable oil
- 2 teaspoons salt
- ½ teaspoon ground ginger
- ¼ teaspoon pepper
- ¼ teaspoon dry mustard
- 1 large orange
- 1 lemon
  Water
- 2 tablespoons dark corn syrup
- 1 pound small white onions, peeled
- 1 cup dried apricots
- 1 cup pitted prunes
- 1 tablespoon cornstarch

1. Trim excess fat from pork; brown on all sides in vegetable oil in a kettle or Dutch oven. Sprinkle with salt, ginger, pepper and mustard.
2. Meanwhile, remove the thin bright-colored rind from the orange and lemon with a sharp knife; reserve. Squeeze juice from orange and lemon into a 1-cup measure; add water to make 1 cup liquid. Stir into kettle with corn syrup and rinds. Heat to boiling; reduce heat; cover. Simmer 1½ hours.
3. Add onions, apricots and prunes; simmer 1 hour longer, or until pork is tender. Place pork on a heated serving platter. Remove onions, apricots and prunes from kettle with a slotted spoon and arrange on meat platter. Discard orange and lemon rinds. Skim fat from liquid.
4. To make gravy: Combine cornstarch with small amount of water in a cup; stir into cooking liquid in kettle; cook, stirring constantly, until sauce thickens and bubbles 3 minutes. Serve with pork. Makes 4 servings.

BOEUF SAUTÉ BORDELAISE

- 1½ pounds ground chuck
- 1 envelope ground-beef seasoning mix
- 1 tablespoon dry red wine
- ¼ pound mushrooms, quartered
- ½ cup dry red wine
- 1 can (15 ounces) beef gravy

1. Combine ground chuck, ground-beef seasoning mix and 1 tablespoon dry red wine. Shape into 4 oval patties.
2. Heat a large skillet over medium heat. Sauté patties 4 minutes on each side; remove from the skillet.
3. Sauté quartered mushrooms briefly in the same skillet. Stir in ½ cup dry red wine; simmer for about 1 minute.
4. Add canned beef gravy; heat to boiling. Return beef patties to skillet for 1 minute. Garnish with a watercress cluster and a tomato rose, if you wish. Makes 4 servings.

3

PENNY-WISE POULTRY

It's simple common sense. When food prices are high, it pays to look for items that offer a great deal for your money. Fortunately, poultry is one food you don't have to search for. It's always available and comes inexpensively packaged in ways to suit every budget, taste and family size. And for menu variety, it's hard to beat. It can be fried, roasted, broiled, boiled or braised, and comes to you invitingly in casseroles, soups and stews. In this chapter we explore some of these ideas using chicken and turkey. Also, since it pays to buy chicken whole and do your own cutting and boning, we've included a page of illustrations to show you how to go about it, plus a list of ideas on other ways to save even more. Add chicken to your weekly menu—you'll be called penny-wise, but no one will ever say you're being pound foolish.

POULTRY: EATING BETTER. SPENDING LESS

WHEN YOU SHOP FOR CHICKEN

• Chicken may come to you packed in over 30 different ways; there's a pack for every cooking purpose and family preference.
Here are some of your chicken choices:

• Whole chicken with heart, liver, gizzard (called giblets) often packed inside. The meat yield for a whole broiler-type is 51.2 percent of the bird by weight. You will need approximately ¾ pound chicken per serving. A three-pound bird yields four servings; a two-pound bird yields two servings.

• Packaged chicken pieces include drumstick, thighs, breasts and wings. One serving is one-half breast, or a thigh and drumstick, or a combination of the smaller pieces.

• Chicken halves cook faster than the whole chicken. They come packed in 1½- to 2½-pound weights. Allow one chicken half to a portion.

• Chicken quarters are convenient and easy to cook. The quarters usually come in 2½-pound packages. Allow one-quarter per person.

• Drumsticks are great finger foods. They weigh four to five ounces each. Two make one serving.

• Thighs are delicious dark meat in convenient form. Use "as is" or bone them for a real treat. They average four ounces each.

• Breasts have the greatest amount of meat of the chicken pieces. They're a good value for the money and so low in calories. A three-ounce portion has only 185 calories or 115 without the skin. Allow one-half breast per serving. Breasts range from 12 to 15 ounces each.

• Wings are great party nibblers. Two wings usually make one serving. Each wing is approximately two ounces.

• Chicken livers are really delicious and reasonable. Allow ¼ pound per serving.

• Choose the kind—whole or cut-up—and weight best suited to the way you want to cook it. Choosiness pays off, too, when your family prefers either light or dark meat, or when you want special parts for a special dish.

• When buying chicken whole, remember these points: Broiler-fryers (one to three pounds) are the youngest, most tender chickens, but they yield the least meat. Roasting chickens, at between four and six pounds are older and less tender, but meatier. Stewing chickens, the oldest and least tender, are the meatiest and most economical. Keep in mind, also, that poultry is graded only on the basis of "U.S. Grade A" or

"U.S. Grade B." There's no such thing as "Prime" chicken. And when it comes to brands, a Grade A turkey is a Grade A turkey. Same for chickens.

• Save chicken livers in a container in the freezer until you've accumulated enough to make a whole meal.

• Watch for specials on chicken, then buy some for today's dinner, some for the freezer. And remember—it takes little extra work to fry a big batch of parts, put a second bird in to roast, or stew an extra one for another day's treat.

• When you get the chicken home, loosen the supermarket wrapping and store in the coldest part of the refrigerator, depending upon its design, up to two days.

TURKEY-BUYING TIPS

• Shall it be a tom or a hen? Both are equally tender, equally fine eating. And there is no difference in the cooking or length of roasting time. Most labels simply say TURKEY, but, in some areas, large toms weighing 20 pounds and over are often advertised as such and are usually priced a few cents a pound less than smaller birds. For a large family or a big holiday feast, you couldn't find a better buy.

• What size should you buy? Giblets and neck are included in the weight of each wrapped bird, so consider this when figuring the size turkey you'll need. Good rules of thumb are: Allow 1 pound per serving when buying a turkey weighing less than 12 pounds, or ½ to ¾ pound per serving for one over 12 pounds. Remember, too, that, since it takes so little additional time and fuel to roast a larger bird, it's smart shopping to buy a big one that'll give you generous first-day slices plus extra for snacks and a second-day dinner treat. If you count on about 1½ pounds of turkey per person, you'll have enough.

• When preparing turkey or chicken, take the wing tips, back, heart, neck and gizzard—any parts your family may not care to eat, and freeze them. Save them until the turkey is carved bare or additional parts accumulate. (You need about four pounds). Defrost parts, cut up a carrot, celery stalk, onion, and add these to four quarts of water in a large pot. Bring to a boil, reduce heat and simmer for about two hours. The result: Delicious, concentrated, versatile stock.

CHICKEN PAPRIKASH

2 broiler-fryers (about 3 pounds each)
2 tablespoons butter or margarine
1 large onion, chopped (1 cup)
2 tablespoons paprika
1 tablespoon flour
3 teaspoons salt
¼ teaspoon pepper
1 can (8 ounces) tomatoes
1 package (1 pound) noodles
1 cup (8-ounce carton) dairy sour cream
1 tablespoon chopped parsley

1. Cut chickens into serving-size pieces.
2. Sauté onion in butter or margarine until soft in a large skillet with a cover. Stir in paprika and flour; cook, stirring constantly, 1 minute. Stir in salt, pepper and tomatoes (breaking with spoon).
3. Add chicken and giblets (except livers), turning to coat pieces well; cover. Simmer 30 minutes. Turn chicken pieces; add livers; simmer 15 minutes longer, or until chicken is tender.
4. Meanwhile, cook noodles, following label directions; drain; spoon onto hot serving platter. Remove chicken from skillet with a slotted spoon. Arrange on platter with noodles; keep warm.
5. Spoon sour cream into a medium-size bowl. Heat sauce in skillet to boiling; stir slowly into sour cream, blending well. Spoon over chicken. Garnish with parsley. Makes 8 servings.

MANDARIN CHICKEN BREASTS

6 chicken breasts (about 12 ounces each), boned
   Salt
1½ cups hot cooked rice
3 tablespoons butter or margarine
1 tablespoon chopped parsley
¼ teaspoon leaf rosemary, crumbled
¼ teaspoon leaf basil, crumbled
¼ cup flour
½ teaspoon paprika
2 envelopes instant chicken broth or 2 teaspoons granulated chicken bouillon
1¾ cups water
1 tablespoon instant minced onion
2 tablespoons lemon juice

1 bay leaf
1 tablespoon cornstarch
1 can (about 11 ounces) mandarin-orange segments, drained
1 cup seedless green grapes

1. Sprinkle insides of chicken breasts lightly with salt.
2. Combine rice, 1 tablespoon of the butter or margarine, ¼ teaspoon salt, parsley, rosemary and basil in a large bowl; toss lightly to mix; spoon into hollows in chicken breasts. Fold edges over stuffing to cover completely; fasten with wooden picks.
3. Mix flour, paprika and ½ teaspoon salt in a pie plate; dip chicken breasts into mixture to coat well. Brown slowly in remaining 2 tablespoons butter or margarine in a large frying pan.
4. Stir in chicken broth, water, onion, lemon juice and bay leaf; heat to boiling; cover.
5. Simmer 25 minutes, or until chicken is tender; remove bay leaf. Place chicken on a heated deep serving platter; keep warm. Reheat liquid to boiling.
6. Smooth cornstarch with a little water to a paste in a cup; stir into liquid in frying pan. Cook, stirring constantly, until sauce thickens and boils 3 minutes. Stir in mandarin-orange segments and grapes; heat until bubbly. Spoon over chicken. Garnish with additional grapes and mandarin-orange segments, if you wish. Makes 6 servings.

CALICO CHICKEN SKILLET

1 broiler-fryer (about 2½ pounds)
3 tablespoons vegetable oil
1 large onion, chopped (1 cup)
1 clove of garlic, minced
1 cup uncooked regular rice
2¼ cups water
1 package (10 ounces) frozen mixed vegetables
2 envelopes or teaspoons instant chicken broth
1½ teaspoons salt
1½ teaspoons leaf tarragon, crumbled

1. Cut chicken into serving-size pieces. Brown well on all sides in oil in a large skillet; remove

Left: For a gourmet-on-a-shoestring dinner, try Mandarin Chicken Breasts, made with an orange-and-green-grape-sauce.

chicken from pan and reserve for Step 3.

2. Sauté onion and garlic until soft in same skillet. Stir in rice and brown for 3 minutes.

3. Stir in water, frozen mixed vegetables, instant chicken broth, salt and tarragon. Add chicken. Heat to boiling. Lower heat; cover.

4. Simmer 30 minutes, or until chicken is tender and liquid is absorbed. Makes 4 servings.

BRAISED TURKEY PERSILLADE

    1 fourteen-pound ready-to-cook turkey (fresh or frozen), thawed
    ½ cup (1 stick) butter or margarine
    2 teaspoons salt
    ½ teaspoon freshly ground pepper
    12 sprigs parsley
    2 cloves garlic
    1 large onion, chopped (1 cup)
    2 large carrots, chopped
    2 stalks celery, chopped
    2 cans condensed chicken broth
      Flour

1. Rinse turkey and dry thoroughly, inside and out. Place turkey giblets (except liver) in a saucepan and cover with water; heat to boiling; lower heat; simmer 30 minutes; add liver; simmer 20 minutes. Remove giblets from water; wrap giblets, except liver, in foil; seal, label and date. Prepare liver in the same way. Freeze both packets for Petite Marmite (see page 105).

2. Place 3 tablespoons of the butter or margarine inside turkey cavity, then sprinkle cavity with 1 teaspoon of the salt and ¼ teaspoon of the pepper; fill with parsley. Tie legs in place; fasten wings to side with skewers. Tie string around middle of bird to facilitate turning. Sprinkle outside of turkey with remaining salt and pepper.

3. Place turkey in deep large roasting pan with a tight-fitting cover; add remaining 5 tablespoons butter or margarine to pan.

4. Brown in hot oven (425°) 15 minutes; brush turkey with melted butter; turn turkey one quarter; stir in chopped onion, carrot and celery. Continue roasting and turning turkey until brown, about 1 hour. Turn turkey, breast-side-down in roasting pan; pour chicken broth over; cover turkey with a double thickness of foil; cover pan.

5. Braise in moderate oven (350°) 2 hours, or until juices run clear yellow when thigh meat is pierced with a two-tined fork. Remove turkey to heated platter; cut off strings; keep warm.

6. Strain liquid into a bowl; allow to cool until all fat has floated to the top; skim off all fat. Pour liquid into a medium-size saucepan; add flour, smoothed to a paste with a little bit of cold water.

7. Heat to boiling, stirring constantly, if flour is added; lower heat; simmer until sauce thickens slightly. Taste sauce; add additional salt and pepper, if you wish. Makes 8 servings, plus meat for 2 leftover dishes.

HAWAIIAN GLAZED CHICKEN

    4 cups cubed white bread (8 slices)
    ¼ cup (½ stick) butter or margarine, melted
    ½ teaspoon curry powder
    1 teaspoon salt
    ½ teaspoon pepper
    1 can (15½ ounces) sliced pineapple in pure juice
    1 broiler-fryer (about 3 pounds)
      Pineapple Glaze (recipe follows)

1. Combine bread cubes, 2 tablespoons of the butter or margarine, curry powder, ½ teaspoon of the salt and ¼ teaspoon of the pepper in a medium-size bowl.

2. Drain pineapple juice into a 1-cup measure; reserve for glaze. Reserve 4 pineapple slices for garnish; chop remaining pineapple slices; toss with bread mixture until evenly moistened.

3. Stuff neck and body cavities lightly with stuffing. Skewer neck skin to back; close body cavity and tie legs to tail. Place chicken on rack in roasting pan. Brush with remaining butter or margarine; sprinkle with salt and pepper.

4. Roast in moderate oven (375°), basting often with pan drippings, 1 hour. Brush chicken and pineapple slices with Pineapple Glaze. Roast 15 minutes longer, basting several times.

5. Stir 1 tablespoon water into remaining Pineapple Glaze in small saucepan; heat, stirring constantly, until bubbly-hot. Serve with chicken. PINEAPPLE GLAZE—Blend 1 tablespoon cornstarch, pineapple juice, ¼ cup firmly packed brown sugar and ½ teaspoon curry powder in a small saucepan. Cook, stirring constantly, until mixture thickens and bubbles for about 1 minute. Makes 4 servings.

HERBED FRIED CHICKEN

      1 broiler-fryer (about 2½ pounds)
      2 eggs
     ¾ cup flour
   1½ teaspoons salt
      1 teaspoon leaf basil, crumbled
     ½ teaspoon leaf thyme, crumbled
     ½ teaspoon pepper
     ¼ teaspoon ground nutmeg
         Shortening or vegetable oil

1. Cut chicken into serving-size pieces.
2. Beat eggs in a shallow dish. Combine flour, salt, basil, thyme, pepper and nutmeg in a plastic bag.
3. Dip chicken pieces in eggs, allowing excess to drip off; shake in flour mixture to coat well. Dip again in egg and shake in flour mixture to form a thick coating. Place chicken pieces on wire rack for 15 minutes to allow coating to set.
4. Melt enough shortening, or pour enough oil into a large heavy skillet with a cover to a 1-inch depth. Place over medium heat. When a few drops of water sizzle when flicked into the hot fat, add the chicken pieces, skin-side down. Cook slowly, turning once, 20 minutes, or until chicken is golden.
5. Reduce heat; cover skillet. Cook 30 minutes longer, or until chicken is tender. Remove cover for last 5 minutes for a crunchy crust. Remove chicken to serving platter or individual plates. Makes 4 servings.

BRIDIE'S REALLY GREAT CHICKEN

      1 broiler-fryer (about 3 pounds)
      1 can condensed golden mushroom soup
      1 leek, thinly sliced (1 cup)
         OR: 1 large onion, chopped (1 cup)
      1 can (3 or 4 ounces) chopped mushrooms
     ¼ cup water
      2 tablespoons lemon juice

1. Cut chicken into serving-size pieces; arrange in a single layer in a 13x9x2-inch baking dish.
2. Combine soup, leek, mushrooms and liquid, water and lemon juice in a medium-size bowl. Spoon over chicken pieces.
3. Bake in moderate oven (375°) 1 hour, or until chicken is tender and richly browned. Makes 4 servings.

CHICKEN DIJON

      2 broiler-fryers (about 1½ pounds each)
     ¾ cup vegetable oil
     ¾ cup tarragon vinegar
      3 tablespoons hot prepared mustard
      1 teaspoon seasoned salt
     ½ teaspoon seasoned pepper

1. Remove giblets and necks from chicken packages and save to make chicken broth. Cut chickens into serving-size pieces.
2. Combine oil, vinegar, mustard, salt and pepper in a large bowl; add chicken. Marinate 2 hours, turning once, in refrigerator.
3. Place chicken, skin side down, on broiler rack.
4. Broil, 6 inches from heat, 15 minutes; turn. Broil 20 to 30 minutes longer, basting frequently, or until chicken is tender. Makes 6 servings.

OLD-FASHIONED CHICKEN PIE

      2 broiler-fryers (about 2½ pounds each)
         Water
      2 teaspoons salt
     ¼ teaspoon pepper
      2 cups sliced carrots
      1 package (10 ounces) frozen peas
     ¼ cup (½ stick) butter or margarine
      6 tablespoons flour
   1½ cups biscuit mix
     ½ cup dairy sour cream
      1 egg
      2 teaspoons sesame seeds

1. Place chickens in a large heavy kettle or Dutch oven; add 2 cups water, salt, pepper and carrots. Heat to boiling; reduce heat; cover; simmer 45 minutes. Add peas; simmer 15 minutes longer, or until chicken is tender. Remove chicken to a large bowl to cool.
2. Skim fat from chicken broth-vegetable mixture; reserve 2 tablespoons fat. Melt butter or margarine with reserved chicken fat in a medium-size saucepan; stir in flour; cook, stirring constantly, just until bubbly. Stir in broth-vegetable mixture; continue cooking and stirring until gravy thickens and bubbles for approximately 1 minute.
3. When chickens are cool enough to handle, pull off skin and slip meat from bones; cut

meat into bite-size pieces; stir into gravy; pour into an 8-cup baking dish, 8x8x2.

4. Combine biscuit mix and sour cream in a small bowl; stir to form a stiff dough; turn out onto a lightly floured board; knead a few times; roll out dough to ¼-inch thickness; trim to make an 8½-inch square; cut into 8 strips, each about one inch wide.

5. Using 4 of the strips, make a lattice design on top of the chicken mixture, spacing evenly and attaching ends firmly to edges of the dish. Place remaining strips, one at a time, on edges of dish, pinching dough to make a stand-up rim; flute rim. (Or, roll out dough to a 9-inch square and place over chicken mixture; turn edges under, flush with rim; flute to make a stand-up rim. Cut slits near center to let steam escape.)

6. Combine egg with 1 tablespoon water in a cup; mix with a fork until well-blended; brush mixture over strips and rim; sprinkle with sesame seeds.

7. Bake in hot oven (400°) 30 minutes, or until chicken mixture is bubbly-hot, and crust is golden. Serve immediately. Makes 8 servings.

ROAST TURKEY WITH OLIVE DRESSING

    1 large onion, chopped (1 cup)
    1 cup chopped celery
    1 clove of garlic, crushed
    6 tablespoons olive or vegetable oil
    3 cups cubed white bread (6 slices)
    2 teaspoons salt
    2 teaspoons leaf oregano, crumbled
    ½ teaspoon pepper
    ½ cup water
    1 jar (4 ounces) small stuffed green olives, drained
    1 turkey breast from a 12-pound turkey (about 5 pounds)
       Roast Turkey Gravy (recipe follows)

1. Sauté onion, celery and garlic until soft in 3 tablespoons of the oil in a large skillet. Add bread cubes, 1 teaspoon of the salt, 1 teaspoon of the oregano, ¼ teaspoon of the pepper, water and olives; toss to blend well.

2. Spoon bread dressing in a mound on bottom of a shallow roasting pan. Place turkey breast over stuffing.

3. Combine remaining 3 tablespoons oil, remaining salt, remaining oregano and ¼ teaspoon of the pepper in cup. Brush over turkey breast to coat well.

4. Roast in moderate oven (375°), basting often with pan drippings, 2 hours, or until turkey is tender and a deep golden brown. Transfer breast and stuffing to heated serving platter; keep warm while making gravy. Makes 12 servings.

ROAST TURKEY GRAVY—Pour off fat from roasting pan into a measuring cup; return ⅓ cup to the pan. Stir in ⅓ cup flour and cook, stirring constantly, for 3 minutes. Stir in 3 cups water and cook, stirring and scraping cooked-on bits from pan, until mixture thickens and bubbles in 3 minutes. Stir in 2 tablespoons lemon juice and 1 teaspoon salt. Gravy coloring may be added for deeper color, if you wish. Simmer gravy about 5 minutes; strain into gravy boat.

YORKSHIRE CHICKEN

    1 broiler-fryer (about 3 pounds)
    3 tablespoons flour (for coating)
    1 teaspoon salt (for coating)
    ¼ teaspoon pepper (for coating)
    3 tablespoons vegetable oil
    4 eggs
 1½   cups milk
 1½   cups sifted all-purpose flour (for batter)
    1 teaspoon paprika
    1 teaspoon salt (for batter)
    ¼ teaspoon pepper (for batter)
    3 tablespoons butter or margarine, melted

1. Cut chicken into serving-size pieces. Combine the flour, salt and pepper for coating in a plastic bag. Shake chicken pieces in bag to coat evenly.

2. Brown chicken pieces well on all sides in oil in a large skillet; remove from skillet.

3. Beat eggs until light in a medium-size bowl; stir in milk. Sift flour, paprika, salt and pepper for batter over bowl. Beat just until batter is smooth. Stir in melted butter or margarine.

4. Place a 10-cup shallow baking dish in oven to heat while preheating the oven to moderate (375°).

5. Pour batter into heated baking dish. Arrange chicken pieces in dish.

6. Bake in moderate oven (375°) 45 minutes, or until golden and puffy. Makes 6 servings.

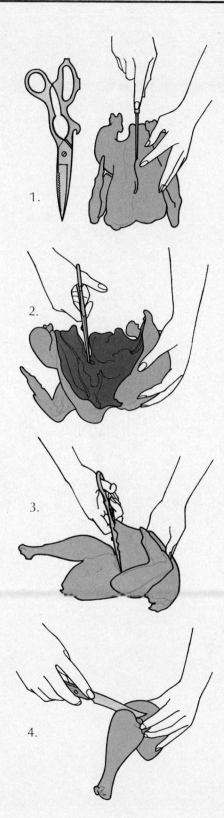

1. Place chicken, breast side up. Using a sharp knife, make lengthwise slit through skin and flesh from neck to cavity. Turn bird over; repeat cut. Then, using kitchen or poultry shears, cut right through rib bones.

2. Turn chicken over. Cut through bones, cutting to one side of the backbone.

3. For quartering chicken, continue using shears. Cut across half the bird, following the natural division just below the rib cage and the breastbone.

4. Cut through joint with a sharp knife, separating leg from thigh.

5. To separate wing from breast, bend joint. Cut through joint with a knife.

6. To bone chicken breast, place breast, skin side down, on cutting board. Cut through white gristle at neck end of keel bone (dark bone at center). Bend back and press flat with hands to expose keel bone. Loosen and remove.

7. Insert tip of knife under long rib bone. Work knife under bone and cut free from meat. Lifting bone away from breast, cut meat from rib cage, cutting around outer edge of breast up to shoulder joint and then through joint. This removes entire rib cage on one side; repeat on other side.

8. Working with ends of wishbone, scrape flesh away from each piece of bone; cut out bone. Slip knife underneath white tendons on either side of breast to loosen; pull out.

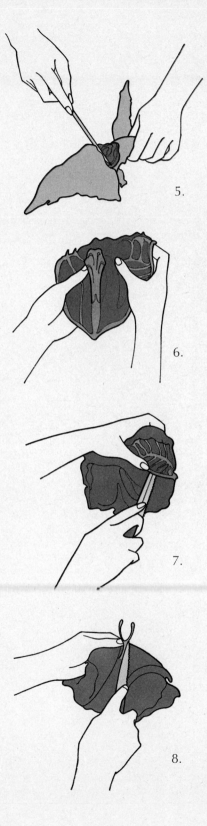

CHICKEN, HUNTER'S STYLE

- 1 broiler-fryer (about 3 pounds)
- 1 tablespoon vegetable oil
- 1 tablespoon butter or margarine
- ¼ pound mushrooms, trimmed and sliced
- 2 large tomatoes, peeled, seeded and chopped (2 cups)
- ¼ cup sliced green onions
- 1 small clove of garlic, crushed
- ¾ cup water
- 2 tablespoons lemon juice
- 1 teaspoon leaf chervil or thyme, crumbled
- 1 teaspoon salt
- ⅛ teaspoon pepper
- 1 tablespoon cornstarch

1. Cut chicken into serving-size pieces. Brown in oil and butter or margarine in a large skillet with a cover.
2. Add mushrooms, tomatoes, green onions, garlic, ½ cup of the water, lemon juice, chervil, salt and pepper; cover. Simmer 45 minutes, or until chicken is tender. Remove chicken to a heated serving platter; keep hot.
3. Blend cornstarch with remaining water in a cup; stir into liquid in skillet. Cook, stirring constantly, until mixture thickens and bubbles 3 minutes. Pour the vegetable sauce over chicken; serve at once. Makes 4 servings.

MANDARIN BAKED CHICKEN

- ¼ cup water
- ¼ cup soy sauce
- ¼ cup dry sherry
- ¼ cup corn syrup
- 2 teaspoons seasoned salt
- 1 broiler-fryer (about 3 pounds)

1. Combine water, soy sauce, sherry, corn syrup and seasoned salt in a small bowl.
2. Cut chicken into quarters. Arrange, skin side up, on rack in broiler pan or in a shallow baking pan with a rack. Brush generously with part of the soy-sherry sauce.
3. Bake in moderate oven (350°), basting with remaining sauce every 20 minutes, 1½ hours, or until chicken is tender and deep golden-brown. Place chicken on a heated serving platter. Makes 4 servings.

STUFFED CHICKEN BREASTS SUPREME

- 4 whole chicken breasts (about 12 ounces each)
- 1 package (6 ounces) process Gruyère cheese, shredded
- ¼ pound salami, chopped
- ½ cup chopped green onions
- 1 egg
- 1 package (2⅜ ounces) seasoned coating mix for chicken
- ¼ cup (½ stick) butter or margarine
- ¼ cup flour
- 2 cups milk

1. Halve chicken breasts; remove skin, if you wish, then cut meat in one piece from bones. Place each chicken breast between two sheets of wax paper and pound with a wooden mallet to thin.
2. Combine 1 cup of the cheese, salami and green onions in small bowl. Place about ¼ cup of cheese filling in the center of each chicken breast. Roll up tightly and fasten with a pick.
3. Beat egg in a shallow dish; place seasoned coating mix on wax paper. Dip stuffed breasts in egg; roll in seasoned coating mix. Place in single layer in greased large baking dish.
4. Bake in hot oven (400°) 40 minutes, or until golden-brown.
5. While chicken is baking, make cheese sauce. Melt butter or margarine in a medium-size saucepan; stir in flour; cook, stirring constantly, just until bubbly. Stir in milk; continue cooking and stirring until sauce thickens and bubbles 1 minute; stir in remaining cheese until melted. Serve with chicken. Makes 8 servings.

LEMON CHICKEN SAUTÉ

- 1 broiler-fryer (about 3 pounds)
- 3 tablespoons butter or margarine
- 1½ teaspoons salt
- ½ teaspoon leaf rosemary, crumbled
- 1 lemon, sliced and seeded

1. Cut chicken into serving-size pieces.
2. Heat butter or margarine slowly in a large heavy skillet; add all of the chicken pieces and brown slowly for about 10 minutes on each side.
3. Sprinkle salt and rosemary over; arrange

POULTRY

lemon slices over chicken pieces and in skillet; cover skillet; lower heat.

4. Cook 20 minutes, or until chicken is tender. (Check after 10 minutes and if liquid from lemon slices has evaporated, add ¼ cup water to prevent scorching.) Makes 4 servings.

KENTUCKY BURGOO

    12 chicken wings (about 1½ pounds)
     1 medium-size onion, chopped (½ cup)
     5 cups water
     1 can (1 pound) stewed tomatoes
     2 tablespoons bottled steak sauce
    ⅛ teaspoon cayenne
  3 ½ teaspoons salt
    ½ pound ground beef
     2 cans (1 pound each) mixed vegetables
     1 small head cabbage (1 pound) shredded
     2 cups instant mashed potato flakes
    ¼ cup chopped parsley

1. Cut apart chicken wings at joints with a sharp knife. Combine with onion, water, tomatoes, steak sauce, cayenne and 3 teaspoons of the salt in a large heavy kettle or Dutch ocen. Heat salt in a large kettle or Dutch oven. Heat to boiling; lower heat; cover. Simmer 30 minutes.
2. Mix ground beef lightly with remaining ½ teaspoon salt; shape into 18 little meatballs.
3. Add mixed vegetables and cabbage to chicken mixture; bring to a boil; add meatballs; lower heat; cover. Simmer 10 minutes. Stir in potato flakes. Remove from heat.
4. Sprinkle with parsley. Spoon into soup bowls. Makes 6 servings.

COUNTRY ROAST CHICKEN

     2 broiler-fryers (about 3 pounds each)
     1 cup water
    ½ teaspoon salt
     1 package (8 ounces) corn bread-stuffing mix
     1 medium-size onion, chopped (½ cup)
    ½ cup sliced celery
    ½ cup (1 stick) butter or margarine
    ¼ cup bacon drippings OR: ¼ cup (½ stick) butter or margarine, melted

1. Remove giblets and necks from chicken packages and place (except livers) with water and salt in saucepan; cover. Simmer 45 minutes. Add livers; cover; simmer 15 minutes; cool.
2. Remove giblets and necks from broth; reserve broth. Chop giblets and the meat from necks; place in a large bowl; stir in stuffing mix.
3. Simmer reserved broth until reduced to ½ cup; reserve.
4. Sauté onion and celery in the ½ cup butter or margarine for 5 minutes in a medium-size skillet. Add with reserved broth to stuffing mixture in bowl; toss until evenly moistened.
5. Stuff neck and body cavities lightly with stuffing. Skewer neck skin to back; close body cavity and tie legs to tail. Place chickens on rack in roasting pan. Brush with part of bacon drippings or butter or margarine.
6. Roast in moderate oven (350°) basting every 30 minutes with bacon drippings or butter, 1½ hours, or until tender. Makes 8 servings.

CURRIED TURKEY PLATTER

     4 frozen turkey legs (1 pound each), thawed
    ¼ cup vegetable oil
     1 large onion, chopped (1 cup)
     1 clove of garlic, minced
     2 teaspoons curry powder
     1 teaspoon salt
    ½ teaspoon ground ginger
       Water
     2 tablespoons lemon juice
     1 jar (about 8 ounces) junior applesauce-and-apricots
     1 jar (about 5 ounces) baby-pack prunes
     1 package (6 ounces) chicken-flavor rice mix
       Butter or margarine

1. Brown turkey legs slowly in oil in a heavy kettle or Dutch oven; remove.
2. Stir onion, garlic, curry powder, salt and ginger into drippings in kettle; cook slowly until onion is soft. Stir in 1½ cups water, lemon juice and fruits. Return turkey to kettle; heat to boiling; cover.
3. Simmer, turning turkey several times, 2 hours, or until tender.
4. Cook rice mix with water and butter or margarine, following label directions.
5. Place turkey in the center of a heated serving platter; spoon rice at each end. Skim fat, if any, from sauce in kettle; reheat sauce to boiling. Serve separately. Makes 4 servings.

4

FISH FOR ECONOMY

All too often fish is considered a meat substitute rather than a permanent part of the weekly menu. This chapter is designed to change all that. First, we tackle the one area that makes many people shy away from this delectable food, the question of how to buy fish—how much, what kind and in what form. On the following pages you'll find numerous suggestions along these lines, plus a page of drawings that shows you the most common market forms of fish. Then it's on to the recipes and, since fish adapts so beautifully to all kinds of seasonings, the possibilities here are almost endless. As for cooking, here, too, fish is adaptable. It's great fried, broiled, baked, poached or steamed. What more could you ask when, on top of all these merits, fish is also a money- saver!

FISH:
EATING BETTER, SPENDING LESS

WHAT TO LOOK FOR WHEN YOU BUY FRESH FISH

Fresh fish, like many other foods, is less costly at certain times of the year—depending on the variety of fish you're buying and the area you live in. Ask at your local market which fish are in season now and which are the best buys.
• Fresh fish may be purchased whole, dressed, in steaks, fillets or chunks (see page 49). When you buy it either whole or dressed, look for the following characteristics: Firm flesh; fresh and mild odor; bright, clear, full eyes (not cloudy, pink or sunken); red gills, free of slime; shiny skin with the color unfaded.
• Fillets, steaks and chunks should have firm textured flesh and a fresh, mild odor.

FROZEN FISH

May be bought by the pound whole, dressed, in steaks, fillets, chunks, portions and sticks (see page 49). Throughout the year you'll see numerous varieties available.
• Look for the following characteristics as a guide to buying frozen fish of good quality: The flesh should be solidly frozen when you buy it and should not be discolored or have any freezer burn. It should have little or no odor.
• Keep frozen (at 0°) until ready to use. Store in its original wrapper. Follow label directions for thawing and cooking.

CANNED FISH

Comes in a wide variety of styles and often offers an economical alternative to fresh or frozen fish. Tuna, salmon, mackerel and sardines are the most abundant kinds of canned fish. Look for the following, all of the same quality, but at varying prices:
• Tuna, Fancy or Solid: A good choice for recipes where appearance is important, such as cold platters, this type of tuna is also the most expensive of tuna packs. Each can contains 3 or 4 large pieces packed in oil or water.
• Chunk-Style Tuna, unlike fancy, is cut into convenient-size pieces. It is more moderately priced than fancy and is good for salads.
• Flaked or grated tuna, excellent for sandwiches or dishes where appearance doesn't mat-

ter, is usually lower in price than fancy or chunk-style and offers the same nutritional qualities.
• Salmon is available in the following grades, listed in descending order according to price—red or sockeye; chinook or king salmon; medium-red, coho or silver salmon; pink salmon; and chum or keta salmon. The higher priced varieties are deeper red in color and have a higher oil content.
• Mackerel and Maine sardines are available in 15-ounce cans and 3¾ or 4-ounce cans repectively. Both offer economy.

STORAGE

• Fresh fish will keep in the refrigerator (at 35° to 40°) for one to two days before cooking.
• Frozen raw fish can be kept in the freezer (at 0°) in its original wrapper, up to six months.
• Cooked fish products can be stored in the refrigerator for three to four days and in the freezer for about three months.
• Canned fish should be stored in a cool, dry place for no more than a year.

GOOD FISH BUYS

Consider the less expensive kinds of fish: Turbot, cod, red snapper, pollock, flounder and haddock—instead of trout, halibut and sole. Also, whiting and ocean perch offer good value.
• Buy frozen fish rather than fresh, unless you live in a fishing area where prices of fresh fish are extremely good. And if you're willing to fillet any fish, you'll save about 50 percent.
• Remember that all white meat fillets can be interchanged in recipes if breaded, rolled, stuffed or topped with sauce. So choose the least expensive for such recipes.

HOW MUCH TO BUY PER SERVING

As a general guide, keep these amounts in mind when purchasing fish:

Whole	3/4 to 1 pound
Dressed or Pan-Dressed	1/2 pound
Fillets or Steaks	1/3 pound
Sticks	1/4 pound
Portions	1/3 pound
Canned	1/6 pound

Golden Stuffed Flounder Fillets is beautifully
at home for family meals or company occasions.
Carrots, onions and bread are used for the stuffing;
on top, a creamy cheese sauce.

TUNA SHORTCAKE

- 2 tablespoons butter or margarine
- ½ cup chopped green pepper
- 1 can condensed cream of mushroom soup
- ½ cup dairy sour cream
- 2 cans (7 ounces each) tuna, drained and flaked
- ¼ cup chopped stuffed olives
- ¼ teaspoon leaf basil, crumbled
- 2 teaspoon instant minced onion
- 2 cups all-purpose buttermilk biscuit mix
- 4 slices process American cheese (from an 8-ounce package)

1. Melt butter or margarine in a medium-size saucepan; sauté green pepper until tender, about 5 minutes. Add soup, sour cream, tuna, olives and basil. Heat just until hot; do not allow to boil.
2. Add onion to biscuit mix, then prepare mix, following label directions for biscuits. Spoon evenly into a greased 8-inch cake pan.
3. Bake in hot oven (400°) 15 minutes, or until golden. Loosen around edge with knife; turn out onto serving dish; split in half. Place cheese slices on cut surface of bottom half; spoon half the tuna mixture over the cheese; put top half in place; spoon remaining mixture over. Serve hot. Makes 6 servings.

TUNA FLORENTINE

- 6 tablespoons (¾ stick) butter or margarine
- 1 medium-size onion, chopped (½ cup)
- ¼ cup flour
- ½ teaspoon salt
  Dash nutmeg
- 2 cups milk
- 1 package (6 ounces) process Gruyère cheese, shredded
- 2 cans (7 ounces each) tuna, drained and flaked
- 2 packages (10 ounces each) frozen chopped spinach, thawed and drained
- ½ cup fine dry bread crumbs
- ¼ cup grated Parmesan cheese

1. Melt butter or margarine in a medium-size saucepan; sauté onion just until soft; stir in flour, salt and nutmeg; cook, stirring constantly, just until bubbly. Stir in milk; continue cooking

and stirring until sauce thickens and bubbles 1 minute; remove from heat. Stir in shredded cheese, just until melted; add tuna.
2. Place spinach in the bottom of a lightly greased 6-cup baking dish; spoon tuna-cheese mixture over the top; top with crumbs and Parmesan cheese.
3. Bake in moderate oven (350°) 25 minutes, or until golden. Makes 8 servings.

COD PROVENCALE

- 1 large onion, chopped (1 cup)
- 1 clove of garlic, minced
- 3 tablespoons olive oil or vegetable oil
- 2 large ripe tomatoes
- 1 teaspoon salt
- 1 teaspoons leaf thyme, crumbled
- ¼ teaspoon pepper
- 1 package (1 pound) frozen cod fillets (not thawed)
  Boiled potatoes
  Cucumber slices
  Chopped parsley

1. Sauté onion and garlic in olive oil or vegetable oil until soft in a large skillet with a cover.
2. Peel, core and chop tomatoes; stir into onion mixture and cook 2 minutes; add salt, thyme and pepper.
3. Place frozen fish block in the sauce in skillet, spooning part of the sauce over fish; cover skillet.
4. Simmer 20 minutes, or until fish flakes easily with a fork. Transfer fish with a wide spatula to a heated serving platter; spoon sauce over and around fish. Surround with boiled potatoes and cucumber slices; garnish with chopped parsley. Makes 4 servings.

SALMON FLORENTINE

- 1 package (about 10 ounces) spinach
- 1 can (1 pound) pink salmon
- 3 tablespoons butter or margarine
- 3 tablespoons flour
- ½ teaspoon salt
- ½ teaspoon dillweed
- 1½ cups milk
- 1 egg, beaten
- 2 tablespoons lemon juice

1. Trim stems and any coarse leaves from spinach. Wash leaves well; place in a large saucepan; cover. (There's no need to add any water.)
2. Cook 1 minute over low heat, or just until spinach wilts; drain well; chop.
3. Drain salmon; remove skin and bones; break into small pieces.
4. Melt butter or margarine in a small saucepan; stir in flour, salt and dillweed. Cook, stirring constantly, just until bubbly. Stir in milk; continue cooking and stirring until sauce thickens and bubbles 1 minute. Stir half of hot mixture into beaten egg in a small bowl; return to saucepan; cook, stirring constantly, 1 minute, or until sauce thickens again. Stir in lemon juice.
5. Fold 1 cup of the hot sauce into salmon. Line 4 scallop shells or 4 individual foil baking dishes with chopped spinach. Spoon salmon mixture onto center of spinach. Spoon remaining hot sauce over salmon.
6. Broil, about 4 inches from heat, 3 minutes, or until tops are light brown and bubbly. Garnish with a slice of lemon and a sprig of parsley, if you wish. Makes 4 servings.

TUNA-POTATO PIE

    1 package piecrust mix
    3 medium-size potatoes
    2 large onions
    1 can (about 7 ounces) tuna
    6 tablespoons (¾ stick) butter or margarine
1½ teaspoons salt
    ¼ teaspoon pepper
    3 tablespoons chopped parsley
      Milk

1. Prepare piecrust mix, following label directions, or make pastry from your favorite two-crust recipe. Roll out half the pastry to a 12-inch round on a lightly floured pastry cloth or board; fit into a 9-inch pie plate; trim overhang to ½ inch.
2. Pare potatoes and cut into very thin slices; peel onions and cut into thin slices; drain and flake tuna.
3. Layer potatoes, onions and tuna in shell, dotting each layer with part of the butter or margarine and sprinkling with part of the salt, pepper and parsley.
4. Roll out remaining pastry to an 11-inch round; cut slits near center to let steam escape;

cover pie. Trim overhang to ½ inch; turn edges under, flush with rim; flute to make a stand-up edge. Brush pastry with milk. Sprinkle with sesame seeds, if you wish.
5. Bake in moderate oven (375°) 55 minutes, or until potatoes are tender and pastry is golden. Cool at least 10 minutes before serving. Makes 6 servings.

FISHERMAN'S STEW

    1 can (1 pound) small white potatoes, drained and diced
    1 cup thinly sliced celery
    2 tablespoons butter or margarine
    2 cans frozen condensed oyster stew, thawed
    2 cans (about 7 ounces each) tuna, drained and flaked coarsely
    1 can (about 1 pound) green peas
    3 cups milk
    2 tablespoons instant minced onion
    1 teaspoon salt
      Few drops red-pepper seasoning
    2 tablespoons chopped parsley

1. Sauté potatoes and celery lightly in butter or margarine in a heavy kettle.
2. Stir in oyster stew, tuna, peas and liquid, milk, instant onion, salt and pepper seasoning.
3. Heat very slowly, stirring several times, just to boiling. Ladle into heated soup bowls; sprinkle with parsley. Makes 6 servings.

BAVARIAN SMELTS

    2 pounds smelts, fresh or frozen (not the breaded kind)
    1 bottle or can (12 ounces) beer
      Fat for frying
    1 cup flour
    1 teaspoon salt
    ¼ teaspoon pepper
      Lemon wedges

1. Split, clean and remove heads from fresh smelts, or thaw frozen smelts. Pour beer over smelts in a large bowl; cover with transparent wrap; chill at least 1 hour.
2. Melt enough shortening, or pour in enough oil, to make a 1-inch depth in a skillet; heat to 375° on deep-fat thermometer. (To page 50.)

HOW TO BUY FISH

Fresh and frozen fish are sold in a variety of forms or cuts. Following is a rundown on the best known market forms, with tips on what you (or your market) need to do before the fish are ready for cooking. Suggestions for methods of cooking are also included.

1. WHOLE, FRESH: Just as the fish comes from the water. Before cooking, have the fish scaled and remove entrails. Then use whole or cut into fillets, steaks or chunks and bake, poach, broil, fry or steam.

2. DRESSED OR PAN-DRESSED, FRESH OR FROZEN: The entrails, head, tail and fins are already removed and the fish is scaled. Normally the larger varieties of fish are called dressed; the smaller ones, pan-dressed. The pan-dressed fish are ready to cook; the dressed fish may be cooked as is or cut into smaller sizes—fillets, steaks or chunks. Bake, poach, broil, fry or steam.

3. FILLETS, FRESH OR FROZEN: Ready-to-cook, these are the sides of the fish, cut lengthwise away from the backbone. The fillets may or may not be skinless. Bake, poach, broil, fry or steam.

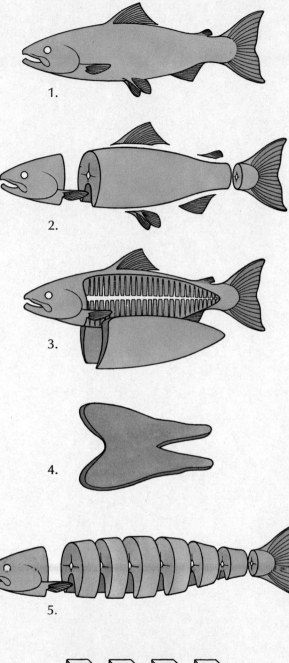

4. BUTTERFLY FILLETS, FRESH OR FROZEN: These are the two sides of the fish cut lengthwise away from the backbone and held together by the uncut flesh and skin of the belly. They are ready to cook (cook same as single fillets).

5. STEAKS, FRESH OR FROZEN: Meat cut from a large dressed fish in slices ⅝- to 1-inch thick. The only bone in this cut is a cross-section of the backbone. Steaks are ready to cook as purchased and may be baked, poached, broiled, fried or steamed.

6. FRIED FISH STICKS, FROZEN: Fish sticks are ready to heat-and-serve when you purchase them (either by deep frying or oven frying). They are cut from frozen fish blocks and then coated with a batter, breaded, partially cooked, packaged and frozen. In addition to fish sticks, you may also find that the frozen food section of your market carries fried fish portions and raw frozen fish portions which have been breaded. Both are also cut from frozen fish blocks and are ready to cook or heat-and-serve as directed on the package label.

3. Combine flour, salt and pepper in a pie plate. Remove smelts from beer with a slotted spoon; reserve beer. Roll smelts in seasoned flour; dip again in beer, then again in seasoned flour.

4. Fry smelts, turning once, 5 minutes, or until golden. Lift out with a slotted spoon; drain on paper toweling. Arrange on a heated serving platter or individual plates. Serve immediately with lemon wedges. Makes 6 servings.

ITALIAN FISH STEW

  ½ **cup olive oil**
  1 **clove garlic, chopped**
  1 **tablespoon leaf basil, crumbled**
  1 **medium-size onion, chopped (½ cup)**
  ½ **teaspoon crushed red pepper**
  ½ **cup dry white wine**
  1 **can (2 pounds, 3 ounces) Italian tomatoes**
  2 **tablespoons tomato paste**
  1 **bottle (8 ounces) clam broth or juice**
  2 **teaspoons salt**
  2 **packages (1 pound each) frozen cod fillets, thawed**
  1 **package (1 pound) frozen haddock fillets, thawed**
  1 **pound fresh or frozen shrimp, shelled and deveined**
  2 **tablespoons tubettini or other small pasta**
  2 **tablespoons finely chopped parsley**
  1 **tablespoon grated lemon rind**

1. Heat oil in a heavy kettle or Dutch oven; sauté garlic, basil, onion and crushed red pepper until onion is tender. Add wine; simmer about 5 minutes, or until liquid is somewhat reduced. Add tomatoes, tomato paste, clam broth and salt; simmer, uncovered, 20 to 30 minutes to thicken sauce.

2. Leave fish fillets in blocks; cut into large pieces. Add fish and shellfish to sauce. Cover; simmer 10 minutes, or until fish is just done (it will look opaque).

3. Remove fish to serving dish; keep warm. Add pasta to sauce. Cover; simmer 10 minutes longer, or until pasta is tender. Pour over fish in serving dish; garnish with chopped parsley and grated lemon rind. Stew may be ladled over slices of Italian bread rubbed with garlic for a heartier dish. Makes 8 servings.

Left: Take frozen cod fillets, cut them into chunks, add peppers, onions, tomatoes and black olives. The result: Portuguese Cod, an out-of-the-ordinary dinner you'll love. The recipe is in this chapter.

PLANKED FLOUNDER FILLETS

  2 **packages (1 pound each) frozen flounder fillets, thawed**
  ¼ **cup (½ stick) butter or margarine**
  2 **tablespoons lemon juice**
  ½ **teaspoon paprika**
    Duchess Potatoes (recipe follows)
  1 **package (10 ounces) frozen mixed vegetables, cooked, drained, and seasoned**
    Buttery Cherry Tomatoes (recipe on page 52)
    Watercress

1. Separate fish fillets carefully; arrange in a single layer on a cooky sheet.

2. Melt butter or margarine in a small saucepan; stir in lemon juice and paprika. Brush part of mixture on fish fillets.

3. Broil fillets about 4 inches from heat for about 5 minutes.

4. Transfer fillets from cooky sheet with wide spatula, layering in the center of a seasoned 15x10-inch plank (see note), or a flameproof platter.

5. Fill a pastry bag with Duchess Potatoes; pipe 6 nests of potatoes around the plank; border plank between nests with remaining potatoes. Brush remaining paprika-butter on fish.

6. Bake in hot oven (400°) 15 minutes, or until potatoes are tipped with golden-brown. At serving time, fill potato nests with seasoned mixed vegetables. Garnish plank with Buttery Cherry Tomatoes and watercress. Makes 6 servings.

NOTE: To season a new plank, rub it well with vegetable oil on top and sides; heat on rack in very slow oven (275°) 1 hour; cool; wipe off any excess oil.

DUCHESS POTATOES

  6 **medium-size potatoes, pared**
  ⅓ **cup milk**
  2 **eggs**
  2 **tablespoons butter or margarine**
  1 **teaspoon salt**

1. Cook potatoes in boiling salted water 15 minutes, or until tender in a large saucepan; drain. Return potatoes to pan and shake over low heat until dry and fluffy.

2. Mash potatoes; beat in milk, eggs, butter or

FISH

margarine and salt until fluffy-light. Cool. Makes 6 servings.

BUTTERY CHERRY TOMATOES—Remove stems from 1 cup cherry tomatoes. Melt 2 tablespoons butter or margarine in a small skillet. Saute tomatoes over low heat, stirring gently, just until skins burst. Sprinkle with 1 tablespoon chopped parsley. Add to plank containing Planked Flounder Fillets (recipe on page 51).

GOLDEN STUFFED FLOUNDER FILLETS

    2 pounds fresh or frozen flounder fillets
      (6 to 8 pieces)
    ½ cup (1 stick) butter or margarine
    1 cup grated carrot
    ½ cup finely chopped celery
    1 small onion, chopped (¼ cup)
    ¼ cup chopped parsley
    2 cups soft bread crumbs
    ½ teaspoon salt
    ¼ teaspoon pepper
    ¼ teaspoon leaf thyme, crumbled
    1 tablespoon butter or margarine
Sauce:
    Milk
    2 tablespoons butter or margarine
    2 tablespoons all-purpose flour
    ½ cup grated Swiss cheese
    ¼ teaspoon salt
    ⅛ teaspoon pepper

1. Thaw frozen fish fillets; pat dry.
2. Melt the ½ cup butter or margarine in a medium-size skillet. Saute carrot, celery, onion and parsley until tender. Toss with bread crumbs; season with ¼ teaspoon of the salt, ⅛ teaspoon of the pepper and thyme.
3. Sprinkle remaining ¼ teaspoon salt and ⅛ teaspoon pepper over fillets. Spoon stuffing evenly onto centers of fillets; fold over to enclose. Arrange in a buttered shallow 8-cup baking dish; dot with remaining tablespoon of butter or margarine. Cover baking dish tightly with a sheet of foil.
4. Bake in hot oven (400°) 12 minutes, or just until fish is opaque. Remove from oven and keep warm while preparing cheese sauce.
5. Make sauce: Drain liquid from fish into a 2-cup measure. Add milk to make 1¼ cups.
6. Melt butter or margarine in a saucepan; stir

in flour. Cook, stirring constantly, until mixture is bubbly; add milk mixture. Cook over medium heat, stirring constantly, until sauce is thickened and bubbly. Add cheese, salt and pepper; stir until cheese is melted. Pour the cheese sauce over fillets in the baking dish.
7. Place dish under broiler 5 minutes, or until sauce is bubbly and lightly browned. Serve immediately, with a side portion of broccoli, if you wish. Makes 8 servings.

POACHED COD, PORTUGUESE STYLE

    2 packages (1 pound each) frozen cod
    ½ cup dry white wine
    ½ cup water
    3 lemon slices
    1 teaspoon salt
      Dash pepper
    1 tablespoon butter or margarine
    3 tablespoons vegetable oil
    1 clove garlic, crushed
    1 large onion, sliced
    2 small green peppers, halved, seeded and
      cut into strips
    2 tomatoes, cut in wedges
    ½ cup pitted ripe olives
      Chopped parsley

1. Remove fish from freezer; cut each block of fish into 3 pieces with a serrated knife.
2. Combine fish, wine, water, lemon slices, salt and pepper in a large skillet; bring to boiling; lower heat. Simmer, covered, turning pieces once, 20 minutes, or until fish flakes easily when pierced with a fork. Remove fish to heated serving dish with a slotted spoon; keep warm while preparing sauce and vegetables. Remove and discard lemon slices.
3. Reduce cooking liquid by boiling rapidly, uncovered, 10 minutes, until it measures ½ cup. Add butter or margarine; swirl skillet until butter is melted and sauce is slightly thickened; pour over fish.
4. In second skillet, in hot oil, saute garlic and onion, stirring often, 5 minutes; add peppers, saute 10 minutes longer, or just until vegetables are tender. Stir in tomatoes and olives; heat 2 minutes. Arrange vegetables in serving dish with fish. Sprinkle with chopped parsley. Serve with crusty slices of French or Italian bread, if you wish. Makes 6 servings.

5
CASH IN ON CASSEROLES

The casserole is many things to many people. To some it's convenience. To the large family, it's the littlest leftover deliciously stretched into an entire meal. To others, it's a lifesaver when busy schedules force dinner into a holding pattern. And still others love casseroles because they hate pots. Added to these reasons for making casseroles, goes one other—the dollar. Nowhere else can so much economy be found under one lid— and it's economy of the best sort. The big, hearty servings beautifully disguise the fact that you're watching the budget. Our recipe for Meatless Moussaka is an example. This Greek classic, made with eggplant, tomatoes, cheese and tangy seasonings, will feed eight people at low cost. What's more, it's easy-to-make. Try the recipe for this casserole and all the others in this chapter. They're perfect answers to a worried budget.

CASSEROLES
EATING BETTER, SPENDING LESS

Careful shopping does pay off. If you save only 5¢ on each meal, you'll save up to $50 by the end of the year. Casseroles offer an easy way to stretch these savings even further. Following are some tips to help you get started.

• Use instant nonfat dry milk whenever a casserole calls for a sauce or gravy with a milk base. It's much less expensive than whole milk, and you'll never know the difference!

• Use tag ends of bread for casserole toppings. Cut sliced bread into tiny cubes or pull apart into crumbs, toss with melted butter or margarine, grated cheese or mixed dry herbs. Then sprinkle on top of your casserole before baking. Another bread idea: Slice French bread very thin, butter slices and place, overlapping, around the rim of the casserole.

• Save bits of dry cereal in a jar, then crush or whirl in a blender for a ready-to-use casserole crumb topper.

• For a quick casserole that still watches the budget, try the following: Heat canned beans in a casserole then top with: crisp bacon or thin slices of ham or Canadian bacon; a sprinkle of grated Parmesan cheese or finely minced onion; paper-thin green-pepper rings; a drizzle of molasses sparked with mustard; heat-and-serve sausage links or thin pork chops.

• For a convenience-food casserole, try this: Start with precooked rice or macaroni, or curried, Spanish or Chinese fried-rice mix. Add one of the following—a can of drained flaked tuna, diced canned luncheon meat or cut-up leftover meat from a roast. Add canned tomato sauce and heat all together in the oven.

• Stir Worcestershire sauce to taste into canned chicken stew; heat to boiling; spoon into a baking dish. Top with a pastry crust flavored with a smidgen of sage. Bake in hot oven (400°) until golden.

• Prepare packaged Spanish-rice mix and place in a baking dish. Arrange canned Vienna sausages on top; sprinkle all generously with grated Cheddar cheese. Bake in hot oven (400°) 20 minutes, or until bubbly hot and cheese melts.

• Leftover meats and vegetables are naturals for casseroles, and they can cut costs dramatically over purchasing special ingredients.

• It's a good idea, therefore, to buy foods with leftovers in mind, to use for casseroles (See our planned leftovers in Chapter 11).

• Use up leftover sauces and gravies in casseroles, combined with vegetables and meats.

SUBSTITUTIONS

When preparing casseroles from leftovers you may run across a necessary ingredient you don't have. The following chart is designed to help you make-do.

IF YOU DON'T HAVE:	SUBSTITUTE THE FOLLOWING:
1 whole egg	2 egg yolks or 2½ tablespoons sifted dry whole egg powder plus 2½ tablespoons lukewarm water
1 tablespoon flour (for thickening)	½ tablespoon cornstarch or 1 tablespoon granular tapioca or 2 teaspoons quick cooking tapioca or 2 tablespoons of granular cereal
1 cup sifted flour	1 cup unsifted minus 2 tablespoons
1 cup honey	1¼ cups sugar plus ¼ cup liquid*
1 cup corn syrup	1 cup sugar plus ¼ cup liquid*
1 cup milk	½ cup evaporated milk plus ½ cup water or approximately ¼ cup nonfat dry milk plus water to make 1 cup fluid milk or approximately ⅓ cup instant nonfat dry milk plus water to make 1 cup fluid milk
1 medium-size onion, chopped	1 tablespoon instant minced onion, rehydrated

*Use the same liquid called for in the recipe.

CHICKEN IN WALNUT SAUCE

    1 package (8 ounces) regular noodles
    2 broiler-fryers, weighing about 2 pounds
      each, cut in serving-size pieces
    2 teaspoons salt
    ½ teaspoon leaf rosemary, crumbled
    ¼ teaspoon pepper
    3 tablespoons butter or margarine
    1 medium-size onion, chopped (½ cup)
    4 tablespoons flour
 1 ¾ cups milk
    ¼ cup dry white wine
    1 can condensed cream of chicken soup
    1 can (4 ounces) walnuts, chopped
      Paprika

1. Cook noodles, following the label directions; drain well. Place in a refrigerator-to-oven baking dish, 13x9x2.
2. Season chicken with 1½ teaspoons of the salt, rosemary and pepper. Brown, part at a time, in butter or margarine in a large frying pan; place in a single layer over noodles.
3. Stir onion into drippings in pan; sauté until soft. Blend in flour; cook, stirring constantly, until bubbly. Stir in milk and wine; continue cooking and stirring until sauce thickens and boils 1 minute. Stir in soup, walnuts and remaining ½ teaspoon salt. Pour over mixture in baking dish. Sprinkle with paprika. Cover; chill.
4. About 1 hour and 15 minutes before serving time, place baking dish, covered, in moderate oven (350°).
5. Bake 1 hour and 15 minutes, or until bubbly and chicken is tender. Makes 8 servings.

CHOW MEIN CASSEROLE

    1 pound chicken breast fillets (boneless)
    2 tablespoons vegetable oil
    3 tablespoons soy sauce
    1 envelope or teaspoon instant chicken broth
    1 cup water
    1 divider pack (43 ounces) mushroom chow
      mein
    2 cups cooked rice
    1 can (3 ounces) chow mein noodles

1. Cut the chicken meat into strips ¼-inch wide.
2. Heat oil in a medium-size skillet 30 seconds. Add chicken. Stir-fry quickly until chicken turns white, about 5 minutes.
3. Stir in soy sauce, chicken broth, water and can of sauce from chow mein.
4. Drain and rinse can of vegetables; stir into chicken mixture; heat to bubbly-hot.
5. Layer half the cooked rice in buttered 8-cup casserole; add half the hot chicken mixture; repeat layering; sprinkle top with noodles.
6. Bake, uncovered, in hot oven (400°) for 15 minutes, or until bubbly-hot. Serve with additional soy sauce. Makes 4 servings.

BACON AND LIVER CASSEROLE

    6 slices bacon, chopped
    1 large onion, chopped (1 cup)
    ½ cup all-purpose flour
    1 teaspoon salt
      Dash of pepper
    2 pounds sliced beef liver
 2 ½ cups milk
    ½ cup packaged bread crumbs
    2 tablespoons margarine, melted

1. Combine bacon and onion in a large skillet. Cook until bacon is crisp and onion is tender. Remove with slotted spoon, reserving drippings in skillet.
2. Combine flour, salt and pepper; coat liver. Reserve remaining flour mixture.
3. Fry liver in reserved bacon drippings; cut into serving-size pieces. Place in 8-cup baking dish.
4. Blend reserved flour mixture with drippings in skillet; add milk. Cook over medium heat, stirring constantly, until the sauce thickens and bubbles.
5. Pour sauce over liver; sprinkle with bacon and onion mixture. Combine bread crumbs with margarine; sprinkle evenly over casserole.
6. Bake in moderate oven (350°) for 25 minutes, or until sauce is bubbly. Makes 8 servings.

TONGUE AND RICE CASSEROLE

    ¾ cup uncooked rice
    1 package (10 ounces) frozen peas, cooked
      and drained
    2 cups cubed, cooked, smoked tongue
    1 can condensed Cheddar cheese soup
    1 cup milk

¼ teaspoon salt
⅛ teaspoon pepper
½ cup packaged croutons

1. Cook rice, following label directions.
2. Combine rice, peas and tongue in a shallow 8-cup baking dish.
3. Blend cheese soup with milk in a medium-size bowl; add salt and pepper. Pour over rice mixture. Toss lightly to mix. Arrange croutons around edge of dish.
4. Bake in a moderate oven (375°) 30 minutes, or until sauce is bubbly and the top is lightly browned. Makes 6 servings.

FAST CHICKEN CREOLE

   3 cups hot cooked rice
   3 tablespoons butter or margarine
   ½ cup chopped green pepper
   1 medium-size onion, chopped (½ cup)
   ½ cup thinly sliced celery
   1 clove of garlic, mashed
   1 can condensed chicken gumbo soup
   1 can (1 pound) tomato wedges in tomato juice, drained
   1 can (3 or 4 ounces) sliced mushrooms, drained
   2 cans (5 ounces each) boned chicken, diced
   ¼ teaspoon leaf marjoram, crumbled
   ¼ teaspoon salt
   1 package (4 ounces) shredded process American cheese

1. Place cooked rice in a lightly greased 8-cup baking dish.
2. Sauté green pepper, onion, celery and garlic in butter or margarine until tender in a large saucepan. Stir in remaining ingredients, except cheese. Pour mixture over rice, spreading evenly; sprinkle with cheese; cover.
3. Bake in moderate oven (350°) 30 minutes, or until bubbly-hot. Makes 4 servings.

SHEPHERDESS PIE

   1 package (8 ounces) heat-and-serve sausage patties
   2 tablespoons flour
   2 cups water
   1 envelope vegetable-beef soup mix

   4 cups hot mashed potatoes
   ½ cup crumbled whole-wheat wafers

1. Cut each sausage patty into about 10 small pieces; brown, stirring frequently, in a medium-size skillet. Blend in flour; cook, stirring constantly, just until bubbly. Stir in water and soup mix; continue cooking and stirring until gravy thickens and boils 5 minutes.
2. Line bottom and sides of a buttered deep 6-cup baking dish with 3 cups of the mashed potatoes. Spoon in sausage and gravy; spoon remaining potatoes in mounds over top; sprinkle with crumbled wafers.
3. Bake in moderate oven (350°) 45 minutes, or until bubbly-hot. Sprinkle with finely chopped parsley, if you wish. Makes 4 servings.

ALSATIAN CASSEROLE OF PORK CHOPS, POTATOES AND ONIONS

   6 slices bacon
   4 loin pork chops, 1 inch thick
   4 large boiling potatoes, pared and thinly sliced
   2 medium-size onions, thinly sliced
   1 teaspoon salt
   ¼ teaspoon pepper
   1 teaspoon caraway seeds
   ¾ cup dry white wine
   2 cloves garlic, lightly crushed
   1 tablespoon chopped parsley

1. Fry 2 slices of the bacon in a large skillet until crisp; crumble and reserve. Trim fat from chops; brown chops in bacon drippings.
2. Arrange half the potatoes in a layer in a deep baking dish or Dutch oven, preferably earthenware or enameled cast iron. Top with half the onions; sprinkle with half the salt and pepper.
3. Place chops over onions, overlapping, to form a single layer. Add remaining potatoes and onions, salt and pepper.
4. Crush caraway seeds; add to baking dish with wine and garlic. Place remaining bacon over top. Cover with a double thickness of foil, then with lid.
5. Roast in slow oven (300°) 2½ hours, or until meat and potatoes are tender. Discard bacon; skim off fat, if necessary. Sprinkle with parsley and crumbled bacon. This is very good with mustard and beer. Makes 4 servings.

CALICO FRANKS

2 packages (8 ounces each) frozen mixed vegetables with onion sauce
1½ cups milk
1 pound frankfurters, sliced
1 cup soft bread crumbs (2 slices)
1 package (4 ounces) shredded Cheddar
  cheese

1. Combine frozen vegetables with milk in a
large saucepan; heat, following label directions.
Stir in frankfurters; spoon half into a 6-cup baking dish.
   2. Mix bread crumbs and cheese in a small
bowl; sprinkle half over layer in baking dish.
Top with remaining vegetable mixture, then remaining crumb mixture.
3. Bake in moderate oven (375°) 30 minutes, or
until casserole is bubbly in center and crumb
topping is golden. Makes 4 servings.

TUNA PUFF

Instant mashed potatoes
Butter or margarine
Salt
Water
Milk
1 can (13 ounces) tuna, drained and flaked
4 eggs, beaten
⅓ cup grated Parmesan cheese
2 tablespoons fine dry bread crumbs
1 envelope white sauce mix
Water
1 tablespoon lemon juice
Dash seafood seasoning

1. Prepare 2 cups instant mashed potatoes with
butter or margarine, salt, water and milk, following label directions.
2. Combine potatoes, tuna, eggs and cheese in
a large bowl.
3. Butter a 4-cup baking dish, then sprinkle
with crumbs. Fill with potato mixture.
4. Bake in moderate oven (350°) 1 hour, or
until puffy and golden brown.
5. Prepare white sauce mix in a small bowl, following label directions. Add lemon juice and
seafood seasoning, blending well. Serve separately to spoon over tuna puff. Makes 4 servings.

OLD WEST PORK CHOPS

6 pork chops, ¾ inch thick (about 1½
  pounds)
3 tablespoons vegetable oil
1 large onion, cut into 6 slices
2 teaspoons chili powder
1 green pepper, chopped
1 cup uncooked regular rice
1 can (8 ounces) tomato sauce
1¼ cups water
2 teaspoons salt

1. Brown chops well on both sides in oil in a
skillet; remove.
2. Brown onion slices on both sides in same
pan; remove.
3. Stir in chili powder and cook 2 minutes; add
green pepper, rice, tomato sauce, water and salt;
heat to boiling.
4. Pour into a shallow 8-cup baking dish; arrange browned chops over rice and place an
onion slice on each chop; cover dish.
5. Bake in moderate oven (375°) 1 hour, or until
liquid is absorbed. Makes 6 servings.

CALIFORNIA TUNA BAKE

8 ounces rotini macaroni, cooked and drained
1 can (7 ounces) tuna, drained and flaked
  coarsely
1 package (10 ounces) frozen peas, cooked
  and drained
¼ cup sliced pimiento-stuffed olives
2 tablespoons minced onion
½ teaspoon salt
¼ teaspoon seasoned pepper
1 can condensed cream of mushroom soup
1 package (3 or 4 ounces) cream cheese,
  cubed

1. Combine macaroni, tuna, peas, olives and
onion in a large bowl; toss lightly; sprinkle
with salt and seasoned pepper; toss again. Stir
in soup until evenly coated; fold in cream-
cheese cubes. Spoon mixture into an 8-cup baking dish; cover.
2. Bake in moderate oven (350°) 30 minutes, or
until bubbly-hot. Makes 4 servings.
NOTE—You may substitute elbow macaroni,
small shells, or ditalini for the rotini, if you wish.

CASSEROLES

OLD ENGLISH CASSEROLE

    8 ounces noodles, cooked and drained
1½ pounds ground beef
    1 large-size onion, thinly sliced
    1 tablespoon flour
    ½ teaspoon seasoned salt
    ¼ teaspoon lemon pepper
    1 can (3 or 4 ounces) sliced mushrooms
    1 can (1 pound) green beans, drained
    1 can (15 ounces) tomato sauce special
    1 cup grated Cheddar cheese

1. Place cooked noodles in a lightly greased 8-cup baking dish.
2. Brown beef in a large skillet; remove meat to a bowl; drain all but 1 tablespoon fat from skillet. Sauté onion in fat until tender in skillet; return beef.
3. Blend in flour, seasoned salt and lemon pepper. Stir in sliced mushrooms and liquid, green beans and tomato sauce. Spoon mixture over noodles, spreading evenly; sprinkle with cheese.
4. Bake in moderate oven (350°) 30 minutes, or until bubbly-hot. Makes 6 servings.

CHICKEN RISOTTO

    2 tablespoons thinly sliced green onion
    1 tablespoon butter or margarine
    1 cup chopped celery
1¼ cups packaged precooked rice
    1 can condensed cream of chicken soup
1½ cups milk
    2 tablespoons soy sauce
1½ cups diced cooked chicken
    1 can (3 or 4 ounces) chopped mushrooms, drained
    1 can or jar (2 ounces) pimientos, drained and sliced
    1 can (3 ounces) chow-mein noodles

1. Sauté onion in butter or margarine until soft in a large frying pan; stir in celery and rice; cook 1 minute longer.
2. Stir in soup, milk, soy sauce, chicken, mushrooms and pimientos; heat to boiling. Spoon into a 7-cup baking dish; cover.
3. Bake in moderate oven (375°) 20 minutes; uncover. Sprinkle noodles over top. Bake 10 minutes longer, or until noodles are hot. Makes 4 servings.

SHRIMPS WITH LEMON RICE

1½ cups uncooked regular rice
    2 teaspoons ground turmeric
    1 teaspoon mustard seeds
    ½ cup (1 stick) butter or margarine
    ½ pound fresh or frozen shrimps, shelled and deveined
    2 packages (1 pound each) frozen cod or other white-fleshed fish fillets
    1 can or jar (7 ounces) pimientos, drained and diced
    1 teaspoon salt
    1 cup dry white wine
    3 tablespoons lemon juice

1. Cook rice, following label directions.
2. Heat turmeric and mustard seeds in butter or margarine in a large frying pan 2 to 3 minutes. Stir in shrimps; sauté 5 minutes; remove with a slotted spoon and place in a 12-cup refrigerator-to-oven baking dish.
3. Cut frozen fish into chunks; cook, turning once or twice, until fish flakes easily, about 10 minutes. Add to casserole.
4. Stir rice into drippings in pan; heat slowly, stirring constantly, until golden. Stir in pimientos and salt; spoon into baking dish.
5. Mix wine and lemon juice in a cup; stir into rice mixture. Cover; chill.
6. About 1 hour and 15 minutes before serving, place dish, covered, in moderate oven (350°).
7. Bake 1 hour and 15 minutes, or until hot. Makes 8 servings.

TUNA-CHEESE IMPERIAL

    1 package (8 ounces) wide noodles
    ½ cup (1 stick) butter or margarine
    5 tablespoons flour
    1 teaspoon salt
    ¼ teaspoon pepper
2½ cups milk
    1 package (8 ounces) cream cheese
    1 can (about 7 ounces) tuna, drained
    ½ cup sliced pimiento-stuffed olives
    2 tablespoons cut chives
    1 package (6 ounces) sliced Muenster cheese
1½ cups bread crumbs (3 slices)

1. Cook noodles, following the label directions; drain and reserve. (Turn to page 63.)

Right: Money-saving's made easy with casseroles such as Shrimps With Lemon Rice. It's a meal-in-one you fix ahead and bake when you like. See recipe above.

Home-style cooking a la France includes
Petite Marmite, left, a main dish soup (see
Chapter 9 for recipe) and Alsatian Casserole,
a hearty meat and vegetable combination.
See page 56 for recipe.

2. Melt 5 tablespoons of the butter or margarine in a medium-size saucepan; stir in flour, salt and pepper; cook, stirring constantly, until bubbly. Stir in milk; continue cooking and stirring until sauce thickens and boils 1 minute. Slice cream cheese into sauce; stir until melted, then add tuna, olives and chives; remove from heat.
3. Pour about ¾ cup of the sauce into a greased 10-cup baking dish, then layer other ingredients on top this way: Half of the noodles, half of remaining sauce, 2 slices Muenster cheese, remaining noodles, half of remaining sauce, remaining Muenster cheese and remaining sauce.
4. Melt remaining 3 tablespoons butter or margarine in a small saucepan; add bread crumbs; toss lightly with a fork. Sprinkle over mixture in baking dish.
5. Bake in moderate oven (350°) 30 minutes, or until bubbly. Makes 6 servings.

MEATLESS MOUSSAKA

2 large eggplants, sliced ½-inch thick but not peeled
2 teaspoons salt
Tomato Sauce:
3 medium-size onions, peeled and chopped
1 clove garlic, peeled and crushed
2 tablespoons olive or vegetable oil
4 medium-size tomatoes, peeled, cored and coarsely chopped (reserve juice)
¼ teaspoon leaf rosemary, crumbled
2 tablespoons minced fresh mint
OR: 1 tablespoon mint flakes
2 tablespoons minced parsley
2 teaspoons sugar
1 teaspoon salt
¼ teaspoon pepper
1 can (8 ounces) tomato sauce
Cheese Filling:
1 carton (1 pound) cream-style cottage cheese
1 egg
2 tablespoons grated Parmesan cheese
⅛ teaspoon leaf rosemary, crumbled
⅛ teaspoon mace
¼ teaspoon salt
⅛ teaspoon pepper
4 tablespoons olive or vegetable oil
⅔ cup grated Parmesan cheese

1. Sprinkle both sides of each eggplant slice with salt; place between several thicknesses of paper toweling; weight down; let stand 1 hour.
2. Meanwhile, make the Tomato Sauce: Stir-fry onions and garlic in oil in a large, heavy skillet over moderate heat about 8 minutes, until limp and golden. Add tomatoes, their juice and all remaining ingredients except tomato sauce and heat, uncovered, stirring occasionally, until tomatoes begin to release their juices. Cover; lower heat and simmer 1 hour, stirring occasionally; stir in tomato sauce and simmer, uncovered, 15 minutes longer.
3. Prepare Cheese Filling while Tomato Sauce simmers: Mix together all remaining ingredients except the 4 tablespoons oil and ⅔ cup Parmesan cheese; refrigerate until needed.
4. Brush both sides of each eggplant slice lightly with olive or vegetable oil, then broil quickly on each side to brown.
5. To assemble Moussaka, spoon half the Tomato Sauce over the bottom of a 13x9x2-inch baking pan; sprinkle generously with grated Parmesan, then arrange half the browned eggplant slices on top. Spread with cheese filling; sprinkle with Parmesan. Arrange remaining eggplant slices on top; sprinkle with Parmesan. Finally, cover with remaining Tomato Sauce and one last sprinkling of Parmesan.
NOTE: Dish can be prepared up to this point several hours ahead of time and refrigerated until about an hour before serving—in fact, it will be better if it is, because the flavors get together better.
6. Bake, uncovered, 45 to 50 minutes in moderate oven (375°), until bubbling and browned; remove from oven and let stand 15 minutes before cutting into squares. Makes 8 servings.

SWISS-TUNA SCALLOP

2 cups coarsely crushed saltines
1 can (1 pound) cream-style corn
1 can (7 ounces) tuna, drained and flaked
1 package (8 ounces) Swiss cheese, shredded
¼ cup diced pimiento
1 cup milk
2 tablespoons butter or margarine
1 tablespoon minced onion

1. Combine saltines, corn, tuna, cheese and pimiento in a large bowl.
2. Combine milk, butter or margarine, and onion in a small saucepan; heat slowly until

Left: Meatless Moussaka feeds big appetites on small budgets. It's an old-world specialty made with vegetables, cheese and herbs.

butter melts. Pour over tuna mixture; toss light-ly. Spoon into a greased 6-cup baking dish.

3. Bake in moderate oven (350°) 45 minutes, or until bubbly in center. Makes 4 servings.

CORNED BEEF AND POTATO CASSEROLE

 1 **can (12 ounces) corned beef**
 1 **tablespoon prepared mustard**
 1 **teaspoon caraway seeds, crushed slightly**
 1 **teaspoon salt**
 ⅛ **teaspoon pepper**
 3 **tablespoons butter or margarine**
 1 **package (about 5 ounces) hash brown po-tatoes with onions**
1¾ **cups boiling water**
 2 **medium-size tomatoes, sliced**

1. Chop corned beef coarsely; place in a 6-cup casserole. Add mustard, caraway seeds, salt and pepper; toss to mix well. Dot top with butter or margarine.

2. Stir in potato and onion mix; pour water over; stir with a fork; cover.

3. Bake in moderate oven (375°) 20 minutes, stirring once after 10 minutes. Uncover; stir with a fork; place tomato slices, overlapping, in a ring around edge of casserole. Continue baking 10 minutes, or until potatoes are tender. Makes 4 servings.

HAM AND BROCCOLI ROYALE

  1 **cup uncooked regular rice**
  2 **packages (10 ounces each) frozen broccoli spears**
  6 **tablespoons (¾ stick) butter or margarine**
  2 **cups fresh bread crumbs (4 slices)**
  2 **large onions, chopped fine (2 cups)**
  3 **tablespoons flour**
  1 **teaspoon salt**
  ¼ **teaspoon pepper**
  3 **cups milk**
1½ **pounds cooked ham, cubed (4 cups)**
  1 **package (8 ounces) sliced process white American cheese**

1. Cook rice, following label directions; spoon into a greased refrigerator-to-oven baking dish, 13x9x2.

2. Cook broccoli, following label directions;

drain well. Place in a single layer over the rice in baking dish.

3. Melt butter or margarine in a large frying pan; measure out 2 tablespoonfuls and sprinkle over bread crumbs in a small bowl; set aside.

4. Stir onions into remaining butter in frying pan; sauté until soft. Stir in flour, salt and pep-per; cook, stirring constantly, until bubbly. Stir in milk; continue cooking and stirring until sauce thickens and boils 1 minute. Stir in ham; heat again just until bubbly; pour over layers in baking dish.

5. Place cheese slices over sauce; sprinkle but-tered bread crumbs over all. Cover; chill.

6. About 45 minutes before serving time, un-cover dish; place in moderate oven (350°).

7. Bake 45 minutes, or until bubbly and crumb topping is golden. Makes 8 servings.

TOMATO-CHEESE TART

 ½ **package piecrust mix**
 1 **cup shredded Cheddar cheese**
 2 **packages (6 ounces each) process Gruyère cheese, shredded**
 3 **ripe medium-size tomatoes**
 1 **teaspoon salt**
 1 **teaspoon leaf basil, crumbled**
 1 **teaspoon leaf oregano, crumbled**
 ⅛ **teaspoon pepper**
 ½ **cup chopped green onions**
 2 **tablespoons butter or margarine**
 2 **tablespoons soft bread crumbs**

1. Prepare piecrust mix, following label direc-tions, adding ½ cup of the Cheddar cheese. Roll out to a 12-inch round on a lightly floured pastry board; fit into a 9-inch pie plate. Trim overhang to ½ inch; turn under; flute to make a stand-up edge. Prick well with fork.

2. Bake in hot oven (425°) 10 to 15 minutes, or until golden; cool.

3. Spoon remaining Cheddar cheese and Gruy-ère into piecrust. Slice tomatoes in half length-wise and then into thin wedges. Arrange, slightly overlapping, in a circular pattern over the cheese. Sprinkle with salt, pepper, basil and oregano.

4. Sauté green onions in butter or margarine until tender in a small skillet. Spoon in the cen-ter of pie; sprinkle with bread crumbs.

5. Bake in moderate oven (325°) 20 minutes, or until tomatoes are tender. Makes 4 servings.

6

PASTA & RICE

They're great meat stretchers, but pasta and rice can also stand on their own. They combine well with so many flavors that an almost endless variety of dinners is possible when you use them. They look festive, too, whether the dish is a simple macaroni and cheese casserole or a more complicated dinner such as Homemade Tiny Ravioli which requires making your own pasta dough. But, like any art, this can be a satisfying experience, particularly if you enjoy puttering in the kitchen. Add a salad and bread and you've got a meal that will satisfy the heftiest appetite and the littlest budget. In addition to the recipes for pasta and rice, we've included some for bean dinners because they, too, offer a great deal for very little. All in all, there are three dozen recipes plus tips on buying, storing and saving even more money on these already economical foods.

CASSOULET

1 pound dried pea beans
6 cups water
1½ teaspoons salt
1 clove garlic, chopped
2 carrots, diced
4 medium-size onions, each studded with 1 whole clove
1 sprig parsley
1 bay leaf
½ teaspoon leaf thyme, crumbled
3 slices salt pork
2 lamb shanks
1 cup sliced celery
1 can (8 ounces) tomato sauce
½ cup dry white wine
1 Polish ring sausage (Kielbasa)

1. Pick over and wash beans. Put beans and water in a heavy kettle. Bring to boiling; remove from heat. Let stand 1 hour.
2. Add salt, garlic, carrots, onions, parsley, bay leaf, thyme and salt pork to beans. Cover; bring to boiling. Lower heat; simmer 1 hour.
3. Add lamb shanks, celery, tomato sauce, wine and sausage. Simmer 1 hour and 30 minutes longer, or until meats are tender. Remove meat from lamb shanks; skin and slice sausage; remove bay leaf. Return meats to beans. Simmer, uncovered, to thicken, if necessary. Garnish with chopped parsley. Makes 8 servings.

CHICKEN-LIMA KETTLE MEAL

1 pound dried baby lima beans
6 cups water
1 chicken (2½ pounds), cut up
2 tablespoons vegetable oil
1 clove garlic, chopped
1 large onion, chopped (1 cup)
1 green pepper, seeded, coarsely chopped
1 cup coarsely chopped carrot
1 teaspoon paprika
2 teaspoons salt
¼ teaspoon pepper
1 bay leaf

1. Pick over and wash limas. Put limas and water in a heavy kettle. Bring to boiling; remove from heat. Let stand 1 hour.
2. Wash and dry chicken. Heat oil in a skillet; add chicken pieces and brown well. Remove. Drain off all but 1 tablespoon of fat from skillet. Add garlic, onion, green pepper and carrot to same skillet; sauté until lightly browned. Add paprika; cook 2 minutes, stirring constantly.
3. Add browned chicken, sautéed vegetables, salt, pepper and bay leaf to limas. Cover; bring to boiling. Simmer 1 hour, or until chicken is tender. Makes 6 servings.

STUFFED SHELLS

32 large macaroni shells (from 1-pound package)
1 can or jar (about 1 pound) spaghetti sauce
1 small onion, grated (about 1 tablespoon)
1 tablespoon butter or margarine
2 cans (4½ ounces each) corned beef spread
3 hard-cooked eggs, peeled and sieved
1 egg, beaten
¼ cup chopped parsley

1. Cook shells, following label directions; drain.
2. Combine spaghetti sauce, grated onion and butter or margarine in a small sauce pan; heat just to boiling; remove from heat.
3. Combine corned beef spread, sieved eggs, beaten egg and parsley in a small bowl, stirring to blend. Fill shells using about 1 rounded teaspoonful mixture for each.
4. Pour about half the spaghetti-sauce mixture into a shallow 6-cup baking dish; arrange shells in a layer on sauce; top with remaining sauce.
5. Bake, uncovered, in hot oven (400°) for 30 minutes, or until bubbly-hot. Makes 4 servings.

WHITE CLAM SAUCE

1 medium-size onion, chopped (½ cup)
1 clove of garlic, minced
¼ cup olive oil or vegetable oil
2 cans (10½ ounces each) minced clams
½ cup chopped parsley

1. Sauté onion and garlic in oil until soft in a medium-size saucepan. Add clams with liquid and parsley; cook over low heat, just until hot.
2. For a special sauce, cool mixture slightly and place in electric-blender container; cover. Whirl 30 seconds. Reheat to serve. Serve over spaghetti, maruzzelle or fettuccine. Makes 3 cups.

MACARONI-CHEDDAR PUFF

1 cup uncooked elbow macaroni
6 tablespoons (¾ stick) butter or margarine
6 tablespoons flour
2 teaspoons dry mustard
1 teaspoon salt
1½ cups milk
1 tablespoon Worcestershire sauce
1½ cups grated Cheddar cheese (6 ounces)
6 eggs, separated

1. Cook macaroni, following label directions; drain; cool.
2. Melt butter or margarine in a medium-size saucepan; stir in flour, mustard and salt; cook, stirring constantly, until bubbly. Stir in milk and Worcestershire sauce; continue cooking and stirring until sauce thickens and boils 1 minute. Stir in cheese until melted; remove from heat. Let cool while beating eggs.
3. Beat egg whites just until they form soft peaks in a medium-size bowl.
4. Beat egg yolks until creamy-thick in a large bowl; beat in cheese sauce very slowly. Fold in egg whites until no streaks of white remain; fold in macaroni.
5. Spoon into a greased 8-cup soufflé dish or straight-side baking dish; gently cut a deep circle in mixture about 1 inch in from edge with a rubber spatula. (This gives the puff its high crown.)
6. Bake in slow oven (300°) 1 hour, or until puffy-firm and golden. Serve at once. Makes 6 servings.

VEAL AND SHELLS PLATTER

1 package (8 ounces) maruzzelle (small shells), or elbow macaroni
1 package (1 pound) frozen veal patties
4 tablespoons (½ stick) butter or margarine
¼ cup olive oil or vegetable oil
1 large onion, chopped (1 cup)
1 clove of garlic, minced
1 cup chopped parsley

1. Cook shells in a kettle, follow label directions; drain; return to kettle.
2. While shells cook, combine butter or margarine and oil in a large skillet and heat until foamy. Add onion and garlic; sauté until soft; stir in parsley, cook 1 minute. Remove onion with slotted spoon; add to drained shells. Pour half the butter mixture over shells, tossing until evenly coated.
3. Cut veal patties in half. Brown, turning once, in oil remaining in skillet.
4. Pile shells into center of a heated platter and arrange veal around pasta. Drizzle drippings in skillet over veal. Serve with grated Parmesan cheese, if you wish. Makes 6 servings.

MADE-BY-YOU RAVIOLI

3 cups sifted all-purpose flour
2 teaspoons salt
3 eggs
2 tablespoons olive oil or vegetable oil
¼ cup water
    Ricotta Filling (recipe follows)
    Homemade Tomato Sauce (recipe page 69)
½ cup freshly grated Parmesan cheese

1. Sift flour and salt onto a large wooden board; make a well in center; add eggs, oil and water. Work liquids into flour with fingers to make a stiff dough. (Or make dough in a large bowl, but it's not as much fun.)
2. Knead dough on board (do not add additional flour) 10 minutes, or until dough is smooth and soft as perfectly kneaded bread dough.
3. Wrap dough in transparent wrap. Let stand 15 minutes. Cut into quarters; keep dough you are not working with wrapped, or it will dry out.
4. Roll out dough, one quarter at a time on the wooden board (do not use additional flour) to a rectangle, 12x4½. This takes a lot of pressure with rolling pin. Repeat with remaining quarters of dough.
5. Shape ravioli, following directions with Ravioli Form and fill with Ricotta Filling. Or: Place 12 teaspoonsful of filling, evenly spaced, on one rolled-out strip. Cover with a second rolled-out strip and cut between mounds of filling with a fluted pastry wheel. (Ravioli can be cooked at once or placed in a single layer on cooky sheets until ready to cook.)
6. Heat 6 quarts of water to boiling in a kettle; add 2 tablespoons salt and 1 tablespoon oil. Cook ravioli, 24 at a time, 10 minutes; remove with slotted spoon to heated serving dish; top with half the Homemade Tomato Sauce and grated Parmesan cheese. Repeat with remaining

ravioli, sauce and cheese. Makes about 48 ravioli or enough for 6 to 8 servings.

RICOTTA FILLING

1 cup ricotta cheese
  OR: 1 container (8 ounces) cream-style cottage cheese
½ cup freshly grated Parmesan cheese
1 egg, beaten
2 tablespoons chopped parsley

Combine cheeses in a small bowl; stir in egg and parsley, blending well. Chill until ready to fill ravioli. Makes enough to fill 48 ravioli.

SHELL AND CHEESE PUFF

1 package (8 ounces) maruzzelle (small shells) or elbow macaroni
6 tablespoons (¾ stick) butter or margarine
¼ cup flour
1½ teaspoons salt
1½ teaspoons dry mustard
½ teaspoon paprika
2 cups milk
½ pound Cheddar cheese, shredded (2 cups)
6 eggs, separated
  Sesame seeds

1. Cook shells in a kettle, following label directions; drain; return to kettle.
2. While shells cook, melt butter or margarine in a medium-size saucepan. Blend in flour, salt, mustard and paprika; cook, stirring constantly, just until bubbly. Stir in milk; continue cooking and stirring until sauce thickens and bubbles 1 minute. Stir in cheese until melted. Remove from heat; cool.
3. Beat egg whites just until they double in volume and form soft peaks in a large bowl.
4. Beat egg yolks until creamy-thick in a second large bowl; gradually add cooled sauce, stirring until well-blended. Stir in cooked, drained shells. Lightly stir in about 1 cup of the beaten egg whites; gently fold in remainder until no streaks of white remain.
5. Pour into an ungreased 8-cup soufflé or straight-side baking dish; gently cut a deep circle in mixture about an inch in from edge with spatula. (This gives the puff its tiered top.)

Sprinkle the puff mixture with sesame seeds.
6. Bake in moderate oven (350°) 1 hour, or until puffy-firm and golden. Makes 8 servings.

BEANS WITH PASTA

1 pound dried kidney beans
6 cups water
2 smoked ham hocks (about 1½ pounds)
1 medium-size onion, chopped (½ cup)
4 carrots, chopped
1 teaspoon salt
¼ teaspoon pepper
3 tablespoons tomato paste
2 cups uncooked macaroni shells
½ cup chopped parsley

1. Pick over and wash beans. Put beans and water in a heavy kettle. Bring to boiling; remove from heat. Let stand 1 hour.
2. Add ham hocks, onion, carrots, salt and pepper to beans. Cover; bring to boiling. Lower heat; simmer 2 hours, or until beans are tender. Add more hot water, if necessary, to prevent mixture from becoming too thick and sticking. Add tomato paste; simmer 10 minutes longer.
3. Cook pasta, following label directions; drain well. Remove meat from ham hocks; return to beans. Add pasta; mix lightly. Sprinkle with parsley. Makes 6 servings.

ITALIAN BEAN BAKE

1 package (1 pound) dried red kidney beans
6 cups water
1 large onion, chopped (1 cup)
1 pound ground beef
1 can (1 pound) tomatoes
2 teaspoons salt
1 teaspoon leaf marjoram, crumbled

1. Pick over beans and rinse. Place in a large saucepan and add water. Heat to boiling; boil 2 minutes; remove from heat and cover. Allow to stand 1 hour.
2. Add chopped onion to saucepan. Heat to boiling; reduce heat and simmer 1 hour.
3. While beans cook, brown ground beef in a large skillet; break into small pieces. Stir in tomatoes, salt and marjoram; simmer 5 minutes.
4. Drain beans, reserving liquid. Combine beans

and ground-beef mixture in a 10-cup casserole. Stir in 1 cup of reserved bean liquid. Cover.

5. Bake in slow oven (325°) 2½ hours; remove cover. Bake 30 minutes longer, or until beans are tender. (Should beans begin to get dry during baking, add some of the reserved bean liquid, just enough to moisten the surface.) Makes 8 servings.

BOSTON BAKED BEANS

    1 package (1 pound) dried pea beans
    6 cups water
    1 large onion, chopped (1 cup)
    ½ cup firmly packed dark brown sugar
    ½ cup molasses
    2 tablespoons prepared mustard
    1 teaspoon salt
    ½ pound lean salt pork, thinly sliced

1. Pick over beans and rinse. Place in a large saucepan and add water. Heat to boiling; boil 2 minutes; remove saucepan from heat and cover. Allow to stand 1 hour.
2. Add chopped onion to saucepan. Heat to boiling; reduce heat and simmer 1½ hours, or until skins of beans burst when you blow on several in a spoon.
3. Stir brown sugar, molasses, mustard and salt into saucepan until well-blended. Layer beans and sliced salt pork into a 10-cup bean pot or casserole. Cover.
4. Bake in slow oven (325°) 3½ hours; remove cover. Bake 30 minutes longer, or until beans are a dark brown. (Should beans begin to get dry during baking, add hot water, just enough to moisten the surface.) Makes 8 servings.

SKILLET BEEF SCRAMBLE

    1 cup elbow macaroni
    1 large onion, chopped (1 cup)
    1 tablespoon vegetable oil
    1 pound ground chuck
    1 can (19 ounces) chunky vegetable soup
    1 tablespoon chopped parsley
    1 teaspoon seasoned salt
    ¼ teaspoon pepper

1. Cook macaroni in boiling salted water, following label directions; drain; reserve.
2. Sauté onion in vegetable oil until soft in a

large skillet; crumble ground chuck into skillet; continue cooking until pink is gone from meat.
3. Stir in vegetable soup, parsley, salt, pepper and macaroni. Heat til bubbly. Makes 4 servings.

FRENCH LIMA BEAN CASSEROLE

    1 package (1 pound) dried lima beans
    4 cups water
    1 pound cubed lamb shoulder
    3 tablespoons vegetable oil
    1 large onion, chopped (1 cup)
    2 medium-size carrots, pared and chopped
    2 envelopes instant chicken broth
    2 teaspoons salt
    1 teaspoon leaf rosemary, crumbled
    ¼ teaspoon pepper

1. Pick over beans and rinse. Place in a large saucepan and add water. Heat to boiling; boil 2 minutes; remove from heat and cover saucepan. Allow to stand 1 hour.
2. Brown lamb in oil in a large skillet; remove. Sauté onion and carrot until soft in same skillet.
3. Drain beans and measure liquid. Add enough water to make 3 cups. Stir bean liquid into skillet with instant chicken broth, salt, rosemary and pepper. Heat to boiling.
4. Layer beans and browned lamb in a 12-cup casserole. Pour liquid over casserole. Cover.
5. Bake in moderate oven (350°) 2 hours; remove cover. Bake 30 minutes longer, or until beans are tender and soft. Makes 8 servings.

HOMEMADE TOMATO SAUCE

    1 large onion, chopped (1 cup)
    1 clove of garlic, minced
    ¼ cup olive oil or vegetable oil
    1 can (2 pounds, 3 ounces) Italian tomatoes
    1 can (6 ounces) tomato paste
    2 teaspoons leaf basil, crumbled
    1 teaspoon salt
      Dash of sugar
    1 cup water

1. Sauté onion and garlic in oil until soft in a large saucepan; stir in tomatoes, tomato paste, basil, salt, sugar and water.
2. Heat to bubbling; reduce heat; simmer, uncovered, stirring frequently, 45 minutes, or until sauce has thickened. Makes about 5 cups.

PASTA & RICE: EATING BETTER, SPENDING LESS

HOW MUCH SHOULD YOU BUY?

The chart below shows how much the most popular kinds of macaroni, rice and beans will make when cooked.

Variety	Uncooked	Cooked
Macaroni (unbroken)	8 ounces	4 cups
Spaghetti (unbroken)	8 ounces	4 cups
Elbow Macaroni	2 cups	4 cups
Rotelle (spirals)	4 cups	4 cups
Farfalle (butterflies)	5 cups	4 cups
Shells (small)	2 cups	4 cups
Noodles (wide and regular)	6 cups	3½ cups
Noodles (fine)	5 cups	5½ cups
Regular white rice	1 cup	3 cups
Parboiled rice	1 cup	3 to 4 cups
Brown rice	1 cup	3 to 4 cups
Pre-cooked rice	1 cup	2 to 3 cups
Wild rice	1 cup	4 cups
Dried beans	1 cup	2 to 3 cups

STORAGE TIPS

• Unopened, macaroni should stay fresh for months when stored in a dry, cool cupboard. Once it's opened, however, it is best to keep it in a covered container. Follow the same advice when storing uncooked rice and beans.
• When refrigerating cooked rice, cover the rice so the grains will not dry out.
• Rice has excellent freezing qualities. It can be frozen plain or with any combination of foods suitable for freezing. It will keep frozen for 6 to 8 months.
• For each cup of cooked rice which has been refrigerated, add two tablespoons liquid. Simmer 4 to 5 minutes in a covered saucepan. For frozen rice, thaw and use same method.

MONEY-SAVING TIPS

• Buy rice in packages from a one-cup measure to a two- to five-pound box or bag. And remember, the larger the box, the lower the cost.
• Toss cooked rice or pasta with diced vegetables, meat and salad dressing for a supper salad.
• Add rice or pasta to your favorite soup for extra heartiness or to make it go just a bit further.
• Combine rice, pasta or beans with cut-up meat or chicken from yesterday's roast, or with eggs, cheese or canned fish for a casserole to pull you through a before-payday squeeze.
• Mix varieties—white with brown rice or brown with wild rice, for a new flavor twist as well as for smart "stretching."

KNOW YOUR BEANS

Learn to know and use different kinds of beans for some great money-stretching meals. The commonest kinds are:

Great Northern—Large, white and oval-shape. They cook to jumbo size and are perfect for soup, baked beans, a casserole with meat, salads.
Limas—Color is gray-white to light green, with small ones called baby limas. Serve as a vegetable or combine with meat in a casserole.
Navy or pea beans—Small to medium and white. Popular for old-fashioned baked beans.
Marrow beans—Plump and white and shaped like a large peanut. Use in soups or casseroles.
Pinto beans—Light tan, mottled with pink or brown. Perfect in all bean dishes.
Yelloweye peas or beans—Small and white with a large yellow-brown spot. Preferred for baking.
Lentils—A relative of the bean family with a distinctive flat round dot shape colored yellow to dark brown. Make them into soup.
Split peas—Either green or yellow. And as their name implies, they come split. Use for soup.
Garbanzos—Medium-size, round, wrinkled and a rich cream color. Excellent in soup and in Spanish, Mexican and Italian recipes.
Idaho reds and kidney beans—Most popular for making chili. Idaho reds are sometimes called red Mexican or chili beans, and are dark red, medium-size and shaped like a kidney bean. Their big brother—the familiar kidney bean—varies in color from light to dark red. Use them, too, for casseroles, salads or a vegetable.
Blackeye peas or beans—Small and grayish white with a tiny black circle "eye." A favorite Southern vegetable.
Black beans—Small and really jet black. Also called purple hull beans. Use in Spanish recipes or as a meat substitute.
Cranberry beans—Red brown, plump and oval-shape with dark brown spots and stripes. Known also as October or Roman beans. Use in chili.

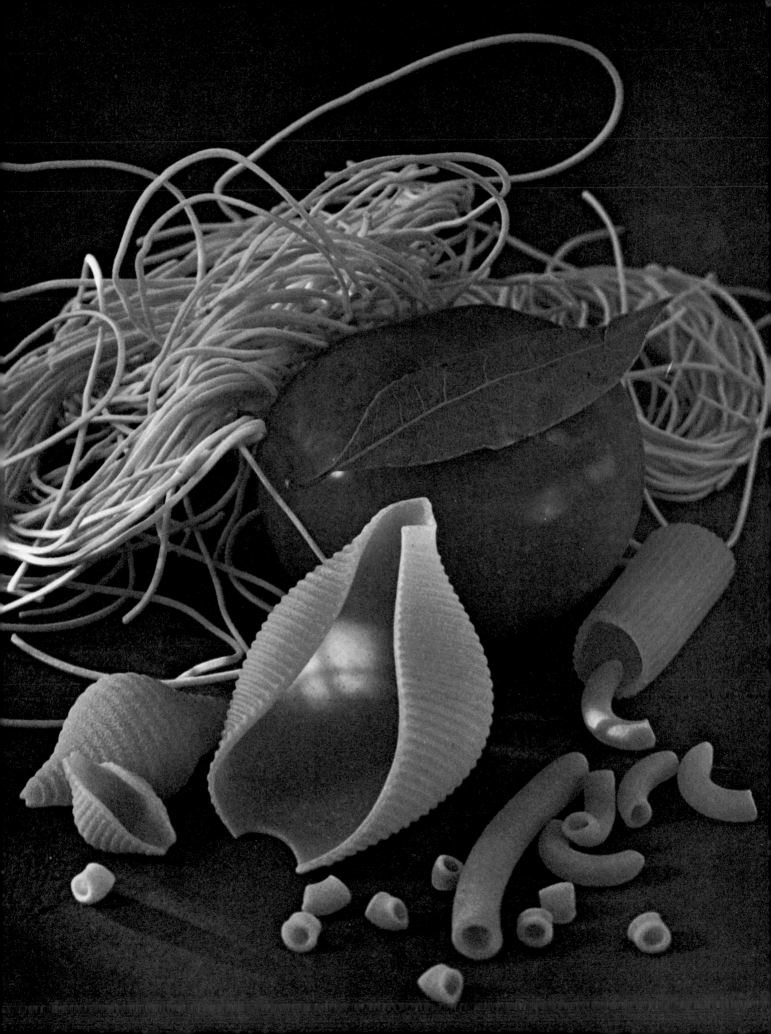

FARFALLE LEONARDO

1 pound bulk sausage
1 large onion, chopped (1 cup)
1 clove of garlic, minced
1 can (1 pound) tomatoes
1 teaspoon leaf oregano, crumbled
1 teaspoon leaf basil, crumbled
1 teaspoon salt
⅛ teaspoon pepper
1 package (8 ounces) farfalle
½ cup grated Parmesan cheese

1. Flatten sausage meat into a large patty in a large skillet. Brown on one side; turn and brown on second side. Remove sausage from skillet and crumble onto paper towels.
2. Drain off all but 2 tablespoons of fat in skillet. Sauté onion and garlic in skillet until soft. Drain tomatoes; reserve liquid. Brown tomatoes in same skillet for 5 minutes. (This is an Italian cooking trick for a tomato sauce with special flavor.)
3. Return crumbled sausage to skillet with liquid from canned tomatoes, oregano, basil, salt and pepper. Simmer, stirring often, 30 minutes.
4. Cook farfalle, following label directions, until done as you like pasta. Drain and place on large heated serving platter. Spoon sauce over and top with Parmesan cheese. Toss at the table and serve at once. Makes 4 servings.

CALIFORNIA CASSEROLE

1 cup uncooked regular rice
3½ cups tomato juice (from a 46-ounce can)
1 jar (2½ ounces) sliced dried beef, cut up
2 tablespoons vegetable oil
1 teaspoon chili powder
½ cup sliced ripe olives
1 cup (4 ounces) shredded Monterey Jack cheese, or Cheddar cheese

1. Combine rice, tomato juice, dried beef, vegetable oil and chili powder in a large saucepan. Heat to boiling; cover saucepan.
2. Lower heat; simmer 30 minutes, or until rice is tender. Stir in olives; spoon mixture into 4-cup casserole. Top with shredded cheese.
3. Bake in moderate oven (350°) 10 minutes, or until cheese melts and casserole is bubbly. Serve hot from casserole dish. Makes 4 servings.

Left: Tiny egg noodle bows tossed with a quick, yet rich, tomato sauce make Farfalle Leonardo a great family supper that's easy on your budget and your time.

HOMEMADE RAVIOLI DOUGH

    4 **cups sifted all-purpose flour**
    ¾ **teaspoon salt**
    2 **eggs, slightly beaten**
    2 **tablespoons vegetable shortening**
       Boiling water

1. Sift flour and salt into a large bowl; make a well in center and add eggs and shortening. Measure boiling water into a 1-cup measure.
2. Mix water gradually into flour to make a stiff dough. (It will take between ¾ cup and a scant 1 cup of water, depending on the moisture content of the flour and the size of the eggs.)
3. Turn dough out onto a lightly floured pastry board and knead 5 minutes, or until dough is very smooth and shiny. Cover dough with mixing bowl and allow to rest at least 10 minutes before rolling out. Makes 2 pounds of dough.

HOMEMADE TINY RAVIOLI

       Homemade Ravioli Dough (recipe above)
    1 **cup ricotta cheese OR: 1 cup dry cottage cheese**
    1 **package (8 ounces) mozzarella cheese, shredded**
    ½ **cup grated Parmesan cheese**
    2 **eggs, beaten**
    ½ **teaspoon salt**
       Dash of freshly ground pepper
    ½ **recipe Homemade Sauce (recipe follows)**
       Grated Parmesan cheese

1. Prepare Homemade Ravioli Dough and allow to rest.
2. Combine ricotta or cottage cheese, shredded mozzarella cheese, grated Parmesan cheese, salt and pepper in medium-size bowl.
3. Divide dough in half; roll out each half to a 22x16-inch rectangle on lightly floured board.
4. Cut dough in half, crosswise; place ¼ teaspoon of filling at 1-inch intervals on half the dough. Lift up second half and place over filling. Cut ravioli with 1-inch round cutter (such as the center of a doughnut cutter). Save dough trims.
5. Repeat with second part of dough and then with all trims to make about 100 tiny ravioli. Place ravioli on a clean towel until ready to boil.
6. Heat a large kettle of salted water to boiling, adding about one quarter of the ravioli at a time; cook 7 minutes, or until ravioli float to the top. Remove from water with slotted spoon and serve with Homemade Sauce and grated Parmesan cheese. Makes 8 servings.
NOTE: Uncooked ravioli may be frozen in single layers on jelly-roll pans and frozen about 12 hours. The frozen ravioli may then be tumbled into plastic bags and returned to freezer. To cook: Follow same cooking directions as for fresh ravioli, but increase time 10 minutes.

HOMEMADE SAUCE

    1 **tablespoon vegetable oil**
    1 **tablespoon olive oil**
    1 **tablespoon butter or margarine**
    1 **tablespoon lard**
    2 **pounds boneless chuck or round, cut into ½-inch cubes**
    ½ **pound sweet Italian sausages, sliced**
    2 **large carrots, finely chopped**
    1 **small onion, chopped (¼ cup)**
    2 **cloves garlic, crushed**
    2 **cans (2 pounds, 3 ounces each) Italian tomatoes with tomato paste and basil leaf**
    3 **teaspoons salt**
    1 **teaspoon leaf oregano, crumbled**
    ¼ **teaspoon freshly ground pepper**
    2 **tablespoons chopped parsley**

1. Heat olive and vegetable oils, butter or margarine and lard in a large kettle. Brown round and sausage a few pieces at a time in kettle; remove as pieces brown with a spoon; reserve.
2. Saute' carrot, onion and garlic in same kettle until very soft; stir in tomatoes, salt, oregano and pepper; return meat to kettle.
3. Heat sauce slowly to boiling; lower heat; cover kettle. Simmer slowly 2 hours, or until meat is tender and sauce is thickened. Add parsley. Taste; add additional seasoning, if you wish. Makes 8 cups.
NOTE: Meatballs may be substituted for the beef and sausage.

PASTA WITH PINE NUTS AND RAISINS

    1 **can (1 pound) Italian tomatoes**
    ¼ **cup olive or vegetable oil**
    ¾ **cup raisins**
    ¾ **cup pine nuts**

Left: Starting at the top and going clockwise are Homemade Tiny Ravioli with Sauce, Pasta with Raisins and Pine Nuts, Maria's Spinach Roll, Pasta with Cream and Saffron, Pasta with Potatoes and, in the center, Pasta with Broccoli. Recipes for all are in this chapter.

½ teaspoon salt
¼ teaspoon freshly ground pepper
 1 package (1 pound) fusilli (spiral spaghetti)
   OR: 1 package (1 pound) thin spaghetti
¼ cup (½ stick) butter or margarine
 1 cup grated Parmesan cheese

1. Heat tomatoes and oil in a small saucepan for 10 minutes, breaking up the tomatoes with the back of a spoon. Add raisins, pine nuts, salt and pepper. Simmer while cooking pasta.
2. Cook fusilli or spaghetti, following label directions; drain well. Return to kettle and toss with butter or margarine until evenly coated. Add tomato mixture and Parmesan cheese and toss until evenly coated.
3. Turn onto heated serving platter and serve with additional Parmesan cheese, if you wish. Makes 6 servings.

MARIA'S SPINACH ROLLS

   Homemade Ravioli Dough (page 75)
 3 packages (10 ounces each) frozen chopped spinach
 1 container (15 ounces) ricotta cheese
   OR: 1 container (16 ounces) dry cottage cheese
1½ cups grated Parmesan cheese
¼ cup (½ stick) butter or margarine, melted
¾ teaspoon salt
¼ teaspoon freshly grated pepper
   Few gratings whole nutmeg
   Homemade Sauce, about 4 cups (page 75)
   Grated Parmesan cheese

1. Prepare Homemade Ravioli Dough and allow to rest.
2. Cook frozen spinach, following label directions; drain very well in a strainer; combine with ricotta or cottage cheese, Parmesan cheese, melted butter or margarine, salt, pepper and nutmeg in a medium-size bowl.
3. Divide dough in thirds; roll out each third to a 22x10-inch rectangle on a lightly floured pastry board.
4. Spread one-third spinach mixture over dough; starting at a short end, begin to roll up dough, jelly-roll fashion; place seam-side down in the center of a triple-thick piece of cheesecloth; wrap cheesecloth around pasta roll to cover completely and tie ends with kitchen cord. Re-

peat with dough and filling to make 3 rolls.
5. Heat a large kettle of salted water to boiling; add one roll at a time and boil 20 minutes, or until roll floats to the top of the boiling water; remove with slotted spoon; repeat with other 2 rolls. Cool rolls on wooden board until cool enough to handle. (This much can be done the day ahead.)
6. Remove cheesecloth and cut each roll into 30 thin slices; overlap slices in a 12-cup baking dish; spoon 4 cups of Homemade Sauce over and sprinkle with grated Parmesan cheese; cover dish lightly with aluminum foil.
7. Bake in moderate oven (350°) 35 minutes, or until bubbly-hot. Makes 8 servings.

PASTA WITH CREAM AND SAFFRON

½ recipe for Homemade Ravioli Dough (turn to page 75)
   OR: 1 package (1 pound) fettuccine noodles
 1 cup heavy cream
¼ teaspoon saffron threads, crumbled
 2 egg yolks
 2 thin slices cooked ham cut in julienne strips (1 cup)
¼ cup (½ stick) butter or margarine
   Salt and pepper to taste

1. Prepare Homemade Ravioli Dough. Roll out to a 22x16-inch rectangle on lightly floured pastry board. Cut dough in half, crosswise; fold each half of dough into quarters, lengthwise; slice dough into ¼-inch-wide strips. Unwind strips and allow to dry on clean towels for 1 hour.
2. Heat 6 quarts of salted water to boiling in a large kettle.
3. While water comes to the boil: Heat cream slowly in a medium-size saucepan; remove from heat. Measure 3 tablespoons of the cream into a cup; add saffron and stir to blend well; beat egg yolks into saffron mixture; then beat this mixture into cream in saucepan; heat slowly, stirring constantly, just until mixture begins to thicken; add ham and allow to heat, but do not allow sauce to boil.
4. Cook noodles in boiling water 5 minutes; drain well. Return noodles to kettle; add butter or margarine and toss to coat evenly. Fold in sauce until well-blended. Turn onto heated serving platter. Makes 6 servings.

PASTA WITH POTATO

    1 box (16 ounces) maccaroncelli or elbow
      macaroni
    1 package (12 ounces) frozen French fried
      potatoes
      Vegetable oil
    2 tablespoons butter or margarine
    1 cup shredded mozzarella cheese (4 ounces)
    ½ cup grated Parmesan cheese
    1 teaspoon salt
      Chopped parsley

1. Cook and drain noodles, following label directions.
2. While noodles are cooking, prepare potatoes, following label directions for frying in oil; drain on paper toweling.
3. Place noodles on a heated serving platter; add butter or margarine, mozzarella cheese, ¼ cup Parmesan cheese and salt; toss until noodles are coated with butter or margarine and cheeses are melted.
4. Spoon potatoes on top of noodles; sprinkle with remaining ¼ cup of Parmesan cheese and parsley. Makes 8 servings.

PASTA WITH BROCCOLI

    1 bunch fresh broccoli (about 2 pounds)
      OR: 1 package (10 ounces) frozen broccoli
      spears
    2 tablespoons olive or vegetable oil
    2 large garlic cloves, halved
    1 pepperoni sausage (about 8 ounces), diced
      (about 1½ cups)
    1 package (1 pound) bow-tie noodles
    ¼ cup (½ stick) butter or margarine
    1 cup grated Parmesan cheese

1. Trim fresh broccoli, removing leaves and cutting a thin slice from the bottom of each stem. Cut broccoli stems into julienne pieces, leaving the flowerettes whole. Wash broccoli flowerettes and stems.
2. Cook fresh broccoli stems in lightly salted boiling water in a large skillet 5 minutes; add flowerettes and cook 5 minutes longer, or until broccoli is crisply tender; drain well. Or: Cook frozen broccoli, following label directions; drain.
3. Heat oil in same skillet with garlic pieces for 5 minutes, but do not allow the garlic to brown.

(This is what gives garlic a bitter taste.) Remove garlic pieces with a slotted spoon; add diced pepperoni and cook about 5 minutes. Add broccoli and brown lightly.
4. Cook pasta, following label directions; drain and return to kettle. Add butter or margarine and toss to coat evenly. Add Parmesan cheese and toss well; then add broccoli-pepperoni mixture and toss them all gently to distribute evenly in pasta.
5. Turn out onto heated serving platter and serve with additional Parmesan cheese, if you wish. Makes 8 servings.

FETTUCINI ALFREDO

    3 cups sifted all-purpose flour
    2 teaspoons salt
    3 eggs
    3 tablespoons olive oil or vegetable oil
    ¼ cup cold water
      Cornstarch
    ½ cup (1 stick) butter or margarine, cut in
      small pieces
    2 cups freshly grated Parmesan cheese
      Freshly ground black pepper

1. Sift flour and salt into a large bowl; make a well in center; add eggs, oil and water. Work liquids into flour with fingers to make a stiff dough.
2. Turn dough out onto a large pastry board. (Do not add additional flour.) Knead 10 minutes, or until dough is as smooth and soft as perfectly kneaded bread dough. Wrap dough in plastic wrap and allow to rest at room temperature 1 hour.
3. Sprinkle pastry board with cornstarch. Roll out dough, a quarter at a time, to a rectangle so thin you can read the cover of Family Circle through the dough.
4. Fold dough into quarters lengthwise. Slice dough across into ¼-inch—wide strips. Unwind strips and allow to dry on clean towels for 1 hour. Repeat with remaining quarters of dough.
5. Heat 6 quarts of water to boiling in a large kettle; add 2 tablespoons salt and 1 tablespoon oil. Cook fettucini 5 minutes, or until they are cooked to the tenderness you like. Drain well and turn out onto a heated serving platter.
6. Add pieces of butter or margarine and toss

with fork and spoon until butter melts. Add Parmesan cheese and continue to toss until fettucini are coated and glistening. For that final touch, grind black pepper over the top. Makes 4 servings.

SPAGHETTI PANCAKE

1 package (8 ounces) fusilli or thin spaghetti
4 eggs
1 tablespoon instant minced onion
1 teaspoon salt
1 teaspoon leaf oregano, crumbled
¼ teaspoon pepper
4 tablespoons (½ stick) butter or margarine
¼ cup grated Parmesan cheese

1. Cook fusilli in a kettle, following label directions; drain; return to kettle; cool slightly.
2. Beat eggs in a medium-size bowl; blend in instant onion, salt, oregano and pepper. Toss with cooled fusilli.
3. Heat butter or margarine in a large skillet. Add fusilli mixture; sprinkle with grated cheese. Cook over low heat about 5 minutes, or until underside is firm and golden.
4. Invert "pancake" onto a cooky sheet; then slide back into skillet; cook 5 minutes longer. Cut into 6 wedges in skillet. Serve with sweet Italian sausages and sautéed red and green peppers, if you wish. Makes 6 servings.

ZITI CASSEROLE

1 pound ziti
1 container (1 pound) ricotta cheese
¼ pound mozzarella cheese, diced
½ cup grated Parmesan cheese
1 egg
¾ teaspoon salt
¼ teaspoon pepper
6 cups Homemade Meat Sauce (recipe follows)

1. Cook ziti, following label directions.
2. While noodles are cooking, make filling: Combine ricotta, mozzarella, Parmesan, egg, salt and pepper in a large bowl.
3. Layers ziti, filling and meat sauce in a 13x9x2-inch baking dish, starting and ending with sauce.
4. Bake in moderate oven (350°) 40 minutes, or until bubbly-hot. Makes 8 servings.

HOMEMADE MEAT SAUCE

1 large onion, chopped (1 cup)
2 cloves garlic, minced
¼ cup vegetable oil
1 pound ground beef
2 Italian sausages, chopped
2 cans (2 pounds, 3 ounces each) Italian tomatoes
2 cans (6 ounces each) tomato paste
2 tablespoons sugar
1 tablespoon leaf oregano, crumbled
1 tablespoon leaf basil, crumbled
1 tablespoon salt
½ teaspoon pepper
¼ cup grated Parmesan cheese

1. Sauté onion and garlic in oil until soft in a large skillet; brown beef and sausage. Pour off all but 2 tablespoons fat in skillet.
2. Stir in tomatoes, tomato paste, sugar, oregano, basil, salt and pepper. Simmer, uncovered, stirring frequently, 45 minutes, or until sauce thickens. Stir in Parmesan cheese; cool.
3. Freeze in plastic containers in measured recipe portions. Makes 12 cups.

TORTELLINI

1 recipe Fettucini Alfredo (page 77)
1 package (10 ounces) frozen chopped spinach, thawed
1 carton (1 pound) ricotta cheese OR: Cream-style cottage cheese
1 teaspoon salt
¼ teaspoon grated nutmeg
1 pound ground beef
2 cans (15 ounces each) special tomato sauce
½ cup dry red wine

1. Roll out Fettucini Alfredo dough, one-quarter at a time, on a pastry board lightly sprinkled with cornstarch, until thin enough to read the cover of Family Circle through the dough.
2. Cut out dough with a 3-inch round cutter. (You will get about 96 rounds.)
3. Press all water out of spinach and drain on paper toweling. Combine spinach, ricotta or cottage cheese, salt and nutmeg in a small bowl. Place ½ teaspoon on each round; fold in half and press edges tightly together to seal and twist into a crescent shape. Continue until all

rounds are filled. (You will have extra filling.)

4. Cook pasta, 24 at a time, in a large kettle of boiling water, to which 2 tablespoons salt and 1 tablespoon vegetable oil have been added, 10 minutes, or just until tender; drain.

5. Press ground beef into a large patty in a large skillet. Brown on one side for 5 minutes; turn and brown 5 minutes on second side. Drain off excess fat and chop into tiny pieces. Stir in tomato sauce and wine. Simmer 10 minutes.

6. Layer pasta, remaining filling and tomato mixture in a 13x9x2-inch baking dish.

7. Bake in moderate oven (350°) 30 minutes, or until casserole is bubbly-hot. Makes 8 servings.

HURRY-UP RICE SKILLET SUPPER

      1 package (about 10 ounces) frozen mixed vegetables
      2 tablespoons instant minced onion
      2 cups water
    ¼ teaspoon salt
      1 can condensed cream of celery soup
1 ⅓ cups packaged precooked rice
      1 can (about 7 ounces) tuna, drained
      2 tablespoons dried parsley flakes
    ½ teaspoon leaf marjoram, crumbled
      1 teaspoon lemon juice

1. Cook frozen mixed vegetables with onion, water and salt in a large skillet 5 minutes.

2. Stir in soup until well-blended. Add rice, tuna, parsley and marjoram. Mix to blend; heat slowly to boiling, stirring constantly.

3. Cover skillet; lower heat. Simmer 5 minutes, or until rice is tender and mixture is creamy. Sprinkle with lemon juice. Makes 4 servings.

CHEDDAR CHEESE SAUCE

      4 tablespoons (½ stick) butter or margarine
    ¼ cup flour
    ¼ teaspoon salt
      Dash of pepper
2 ½ cups milk
      1 teaspoon Worcestershire sauce
    ½ pound Cheddar cheese, shredded (2 cups)

Melt butter or margarine in a medium-size saucepan. Blend in flour, salt and pepper; cook, stirring constantly, just until bubbly. Stir in milk;

continue cooking and stirring until sauce thickens and bubbles 1 minute. Stir in cheese and Worcestershire sauce until cheese is melted. Serve with Manicotti Alla Veneziana (see page 80). Makes about 2½ cups.

ZUCCHINI-TOMATO SAUCE

      1 large onion, chopped (1 cup)
      1 clove of garlic, minced
      1 pound zucchini, trimmed and chopped
    ¼ cup olive oil or vegetable oil
      2 large ripe tomatoes, peeled and chopped
      2 teaspoons leaf basil, crumbled
1 ½ teaspoons salt
    ¼ teaspoon pepper
      Dash of sugar

1. Sauté onion, garlic and zucchini in oil until soft in a medium-size saucepan; stir in tomatoes, basil, salt, pepper and sugar.

2. Heat to bubbling; simmer 30 minutes, or until sauce thickens slightly. Serve over fettuccelle or spaghetti. Makes 3 cups.

RIGATI-EGGPLANT BAKE

      1 large eggplant, weighing about 2 pounds
    ½ cup olive oil or vegetable oil
      1 package (1 pound) rigati, or ziti, or elbow macaroni
      1 large onion, chopped (1 cup)
      1 jar (24 ounces) marinara sauce
      1 container (1 pound) cream-style cottage cheese
    ½ cup chopped parsley
      1 teaspoon Italian seasoning
      1 package (6 ounces) sliced provolone cheese

1. Trim ends from eggplant; cut into ½-inch slices; pare. Sauté slices, a few at a time, in part of the oil, until soft in a large skillet; drain on paper toweling.

2. Cook rigati in a kettle, following label directions; drain; return to kettle.

3. Sauté onion until soft in same skillet; stir in marinara sauce and simmer until piping-hot. Pour sauce over rigati in kettle and blend well.

4. Combine cottage cheese, parsley and Italian seasoning in a small bowl.

5. Place half the rigati mixture in a shallow 12-cup baking dish. Add half the eggplant, over-

lapping slices if necessary. Add cheese mixture, spreading evenly. Add remaining rigati mixture and top with remaining eggplant.
6. Bake in moderate oven (350°) 20 minutes. Cut provolone cheese into strips and arrange over eggplant.
7. Bake 10 minutes longer, or until cheese melts and the rigati mixture is bubbly-hot. Serve right from baking dish. Makes 8 servings.

GENOESE NOODLES

    1 package (1 pound) noodles
    ½ cup (1 stick) butter or margarine, melted
    2 cups parsley leaves, pressed down
    1 tablespoon leaf basil
1 ½ teaspoons salt
    ¼ teaspoon pepper
    1 clove garlic
    2 tablespoons pine nuts (pignoli)
    ½ cup olive or vegetable oil
    ½ cup grated Parmesan cheese

1. Cook and drain noodles, following label directions; place on a heated platter.
2. While noodles cook, combine butter or margarine, parsley, basil, salt, pepper, garlic, nuts, oil and cheese in container of electric blender to make sauce. Whirl at high speed until smooth.
3. Pour sauce over noodles; toss lightly. Serve immediately. Makes 8 servings.

SPAGHETTI CARBONARA

    1 pound spaghetti
    ½ pound sliced bacon, diced
    1 large green pepper, halved, seeded and diced
    3 eggs
    ½ teaspoon leaf marjoram, crumbled
    ½ teaspoon salt
    Dash of pepper
    4 tablespoons (½ stick) butter or margarine
    1 cup grated Romano cheese

1. Cook spaghetti in boiling salted water; following label directions; drain and place on heated serving platter.
2. While pasta cooks, fry bacon until crisp in a skillet. Remove with a slotted spoon to paper toweling. Drain off all but 2 tablespoons bacon fat from skillet. Saute green pepper in skillet until soft.
3. Beat eggs in a small bowl. Stir in marjoram, salt and pepper.
4. Toss butter or margarine with hot spaghetti until melted. Add seasoned eggs and toss until completely blended. Add bacon, green pepper and grated cheese. Toss once more and serve at once. Makes 6 servings.

MANICOTTI ALLA VENEZIANA

    1 package (8 ounces) manicotti noodles
    1 pound meat-loaf mixture
    1 large onion, chopped (1 cup)
    1 clove of garlic, minced
    1 cup fresh bread crumbs (2 slices)
    1 egg, beaten
    ½ cup chopped parsley
    1 teaspoon leaf basil, crumbled
    1 teaspoon salt
    Dash of pepper
    Cheddar Cheese Sauce (recipe on page 79)

1. Cook manicotti noodles, a few at a time, following label directions; lift out carefully with a slotted spoon; place in a large bowl of cold water until ready to use.
2. Shape meat-loaf mixture into a large patty in a large skillet; brown 5 minutes on each side, then break up into small pieces; remove with a slotted spoon to a medium-size bowl.
3. Saute onion and garlic until soft in drippings in skillet. Add to cooked meat with bread crumbs, egg, parsley, basil, salt and pepper, mixing until well-blended.
4. Lift manicotti noodles from water, one at a time; drain well. Fill each with part of the meat mixture, using a long-handled spoon.
5. Pour half the hot Cheddar Cheese Sauce into the bottom of a shallow 12-cup flameproof dish. Place filled manicotti over cheese sauce. Top with remaining sauce.
6. Broil, 4 inches from heat, 5 minutes, or until golden and bubbly. Makes 6 to 8 servings.
NOTE: Manicotti Alla Veneziana can be made early in the day and refrigerated. About 45 minutes before serving time, warm in moderate oven (350°) 30 minutes, then place under broiler until golden and bubbly.

7

CHEESE & EGG DISHES

Cheese and eggs offer big protein for little money. What's more, each can be used in an almost unlimited number of ways for either breakfast, lunch or dinner. Eggs, for instance, are one of the few foods that, without adding any other ingredient, can be made into a nutritional main course. And they can be cooked almost anyway you like—fried, baked, poached, soft-boiled or scrambled. Add leftovers and you've got the makings for a satisfying omelet. Add cheese and you've got a combination that's unbeatable in soufflés, casseroles, blintzes, etc. If you've been limiting eggs to breakfast and cheese to lunchtime sandwiches, take a look at the following nine pages. They include delightful dinner recipes and sage advice on getting the most for your money, plus tips on storing and cooking these around-the-clock foods.

CHEESE & EGGS: EATING BETTER, SPENDING LESS

MONEY-SAVING EGG TIPS

• What determines the price of eggs? Weight, among other things. For example: One dozen eggs in a carton marked EXTRA-LARGE must weigh, according to government standards, 27 ounces; those marked LARGE, 24 ounces; MEDIUM, 21 ounces; and SMALL, 18 ounces. Weight is not listed on the carton, but the size is, and that's your guarantee.

• How to figure cost per serving: Divide 12 into the cost per dozen. For example, if a dozen eggs cost 90¢, each egg actually cost 7.5¢. Therefore, an average 2-egg serving will cost you only 15¢. Nutritionists say that in buying a dozen large eggs at 90¢, the shopper is paying 60¢ a pound for high quality protein; eggs are a bargain.

• Egg Grades: Most supermarkets carry both AA and Grade A eggs and sometimes Grade B. All have the same nutritive value. The difference is in the appearance. The Grade B egg usually has a thinner white and a flatter yolk. Regardless of the size of the egg, AA and A grades are perfect for poaching, frying and cooking in the shell and, of course, are the highest priced. Grade B—at a lower price—is a smart buy for scrambling, making omelets or for use in any recipe where perfect appearance doesn't matter.

• When checking the prices of eggs of the same grade, but different size, keep this formula in mind: If the difference in the price per dozen between medium and large eggs of the same grade is 7¢ or more, the medium size is the better buy per pound. If the difference is 6¢ or less, the larger size egg is the better buy.

• Brown-shell eggs versus white-shell eggs. Both have the same nutritional quality and, depending on size, should be priced comparably. The color is determined by the breed of hen. Brown-shell eggs are preferred in some parts of our country; white shells, in other regions. Smart shoppers buy either or both.

• Do not wash eggs until you're ready to use them, otherwise you remove the shell film that helps keep them fresh. Store them in the refrigerator, as soon as you come home from the supermarket. The tote-home carton is fine for storage and provides a light covering. If you change the eggs to a special compartment in your refrigerator, place them large end up.

• If an egg is ruined because of improper cooking, it's money thrown away. Whatever your favorite way of cooking eggs, use low heat.

• Eggs tend to be most plentiful, and thus lower in price, during the winter. So, wintertime is often a time to think of main dishes from eggs.

• Save egg whites. Keep them chilled in a covered jar in the refrigerator. They will keep from 7 to 10 days. Beat whites with sugar until stiff, and use as a garnish for puddings.

• Save egg yolks. Place them in a covered jar with just enough water to cover; chill. Plan to use them within 2 to 3 days. Or poach the yolks right away, then rice them and use for garnishing salads. You can also hard-cook the yolks and store in a covered container for 4 to 5 days. Hard-cooked, they're perfect, mixed with mayonnaise, as a sandwich filling.

• The 2-egg omelet is one of the easiest, thriftiest ways to use any leftover meats, cheeses and vegetables.

MONEY-SAVING CHEESE TIPS

• To find the relative cost of various cheeses, compare the price of equal weights of cheese. As a general rule, you'll find aged or sharp natural cheeses usually cost more than mild ones; imported cheeses frequently cost more than domestic ones; and pre-packaged, sliced, cubed or grated cheeses may cost more than wedges or sticks. Also, large packages are usually your thriftiest buy.

• Save small or end pieces of cheese for garnishes. If the pieces become hard and dry, grate them and refrigerate in a covered container.

• If mold appears on natural cheeses, scrape it off. It's harmless and does not affect the taste of the cheese.

• Try cottage cheese and chives as a change from sour cream as a topping for baked potatoes. It's less expensive and has fewer calories.

• Cheese (except cottage, cream and Neufchâtel cheeses) tastes best when served at room temperature. Remove from refrigerator about 30 to 60 minutes before serving. However, cut off only what you plan to use; wrap and return the remainder to the refrigerator. Warm air only dries out cheese.

• Remember two points when cooking with cheese: Use low heat and avoid overcooking. Otherwise cheese will become stringy or tough —and could be the ruination of an otherwise good dinner. This is true whether the cheese is baked, broiled or cooked on top of the range.

Dinner can be fast, easy *and* economical
with Basque Piperade, an egg-vegetable
dinner sure to please even finicky eaters.

BASQUE PIPERADE

  1 medium-size onion, sliced
  1 medium-size green pepper, slivered
  1 clove garlic, halved
  ¼ cup olive or vegetable oil
  2 medium-size firm red tomatoes
1 ½ teaspoons salt
  ¼ teaspoon crumbled leaf oregano
  ¼ teaspoon crumbled leaf basil
  ¼ teaspoon pepper
  8 eggs
  2 tablespoons butter or margarine

1. Sauté onion, green pepper and garlic in oil in a large skillet until soft, about 3 minutes; remove garlic.
2. Cut tomatoes into wedges; add to skillet, along with ½ teaspoon of salt, oregano, basil and pepper. Cook 3 minutes longer; remove to large bowl.
3. Beat eggs with remaining 1 teaspoon salt in large bowl until blended; melt butter or margarine in skillet; pour in eggs; stir quickly with fork until eggs are almost set. Put warm vegetable mixture into soft top layer of eggs. Do not stir. Cook until edges of eggs are set. Cut; serve. Makes 6 servings.

ENGLISH COUNTRY CASSEROLE

4 large potatoes (2 pounds)
2 tablespoons butter or margarine
¼ cup milk
½ teaspoon salt
¼ teaspoon pepper
2 large onions, peeled and sliced
2 tablespoons vegetable oil
1 cup diced cooked ham
1 package (10 ounces) Cheddar cheese

1. Pare and quarter potatoes. Cook in boiling salted water until tender in a large saucepan; drain potatoes and return to saucepan. Toss pan gently over heat to fluff-dry potatoes.
2. Add butter or margarine and milk to saucepan; heat to boiling; remove pan from heat; mash and then beat potatoes until very smooth; season with salt and pepper.
3. Sauté onion rings in oil until soft in a skillet; add diced ham and sauté several minutes. Cut Cheddar cheese into thin slices. (To page 87.)

4. Spread half of potato mixture in the bottom of a 6-cup baking dish; spoon onion and ham mixture over. Lay half the cheese slices over; top with remaining mashed potatoes. Arrange remaining cheese slices on top.

5. Bake in hot oven (400°) 20 minutes, or until casserole is piping-hot. Makes 4 servings.

THIRTY-MINUTE PIZZA

    Vegetable oil
 4 packages (8 ounces each) refrigerated cres-
    cent dinner rolls
 1 can (15 ounces) spaghetti sauce
 1 can (about 3 or 4 ounces) sliced mushrooms,
    drained
 ½ cup sliced pitted ripe olives
 1 teaspoon leaf oregano, crumbled
 1 package (8 ounces) mozzarella cheese,
    shredded
 2 packages (8 ounces each) brown 'n' serve
    sausages

1. Lightly oil two 14-inch round pizza pans. Open crescent rolls following label directions. Unroll and separate dough triangles. Fit triangles from 2 packages into each pizza pan.

2. Spread half of spaghetti sauce on each pizza Divide mushrooms and olives evenly over sauce; sprinkle with oregano. Sprinkle cheese over both pizzas.

3. Slice sausages diagonally; arrange in a pattern on the cheese.

4. Bake in a hot oven (400°) 20 minutes, or until crusts are golden brown. Garnish with a sprig of fresh basil or parsley, if you wish. Makes two 14-inch pies.

TO REHEAT FROZEN PIZZA: Bake at 400° for 30 minutes, or until filling is bubbly.

SOUFFLÉED BROCCOLI ROULADE

 4 tablespoons (½ stick) butter or margarine
 ½ cup flour
 ½ teaspoon salt
 2 cups milk
 4 eggs, separated
 2 packages frozen broccoli
 ¾ cup shredded Swiss cheese
    Swiss Cheese Sauce (recipe follows)

1. Grease a 15x10x1-inch jelly-roll pan; line with wax paper; grease paper; dust with flour.

2. Melt butter or margarine in a medium-size saucepan. Off heat, blend in flour and salt; stir in milk. Cook, stirring constantly, until mixture is very thick.

3. Beat egg whites until they form soft peaks in a medium-size bowl. Beat egg yolks slightly in a large bowl. Slowly beat hot mixture into egg yolks, until blended. Fold beaten egg whites into egg yolks until no streaks of yellow remain. Spread evenly in pan.

4. Bake in moderate oven (325°) 45 minutes, or until golden and top springs back when touched.

5. While omelet roll bakes, cook broccoli, following label directions; drain; cut into 1-inch pieces. Reserve ½ cup for garnish.

6. Make Swiss Cheese Sauce.

7. Remove omelet roll from pan this way: Loosen around edges with spatula; cover with wax paper or foil. Place a large cooky sheet or tray on top, then quickly turn upside down. Lift pan; peel paper.

8. Arrange broccoli in a single layer on top of roll; sprinkle with cheese and drizzle ½ cup hot cheese sauce over. Starting at a 10-inch end, roll up omelet, jelly-roll fashion, lifting wax paper or foil as you roll to steady and guide it.

9. Lift roll onto a heated large serving platter with two wide spatulas. Drizzle about ½ cup more sauce over roll and garnish with broccoli.

10. Cut roll into thick slices. Pass remaining sauce to spoon over. Makes 6 servings.

SWISS CHEESE SAUCE

 ⅓ cup butter or margarine
 ⅓ cup flour
 ½ teaspoon salt
 ⅛ teaspoon pepper
 2 cups milk
 ¾ cup shredded Swiss cheese

1. Melt butter or margarine over low heat in a medium-size saucepan. Stir in flour, salt and pepper; cook, stirring constantly, just until mixture bubbles.

2. Stir in milk; continue cooking and stirring until sauce thickens and bubbles 1 minute; stir in cheese until melted. Keep warm. Makes 2½ cups, or enough for 6 servings of Souffléed Broccoli Roulade.

Left: Thirty-Minute Pizza is a quick version of a Neapolitan favorite. It's made with plenty of cheese and a big slice of convenience. See above for the recipe.

ITALIAN FRITTATA

- ½ cup chopped green pepper
- 1 medium-size onion, chopped (½ cup)
- 4 tablespoons (½ stick) butter or margarine
- 1 large tomato, peeled and chopped
- 1 teaspoon salt
- ¼ teaspoon leaf oregano, crumbled
- 8 eggs
- ⅛ teaspoon pepper
- 2 ounces (2 slices) Provolone cheese (from a 6-ounce package), shredded

1. Sauté green pepper and onion in 2 tablespoons of the butter or margarine until soft, about 5 minutes, in a small skillet. Add tomato, ½ teaspoon of the salt and oregano. Cook slowly, 10 minutes, stirring occasionally, until all liquid is absorbed; reserve.
2. Beat eggs slightly in a medium-size bowl with remaining ½ teaspoon salt and pepper.
3. Heat a 10-inch skillet for 5 seconds. With a fork, swirl the remaining 2 tablespoons butter or margarine over bottom and sides of pan.
4. Pour in egg mixture. Cook, stirring with flat of fork and shaking pan back and forth until omelet is firm on bottom and almost set on top. Spread tomato mixture evenly over top. Sprinkle with cheese; cover skillet for about 2 minutes, or until cheese starts to melt. Cut in wedges to serve. Makes 4 servings.

CALICO CHEESE CASSEROLE

- 1 package (8 ounces) spaghetti
- 1 package (10 ounces) frozen mixed vegetables
- 6 tablespoons (¾ stick) butter or margarine
- 1½ cups soft white bread crumbs (3 slices)
- 4 tablespoons flour
- 1 teaspoon salt
- 3 cups milk
- 1 tablespoon prepared mustard
- 3 cups shredded sharp Cheddar cheese (¾ pound)
- 4 hard-cooked eggs, shelled and sliced

1. Break spaghetti into 3-inch pieces. Cook spaghetti and frozen mixed vegetables in separate saucepans, following label directions for each; drain well and return to saucepan spaghetti was cooked in.

2. Melt butter or margarine in a medium-size saucepan; measure 2 tablespoons into a small bowl and toss with bread crumbs.
3. Stir flour and salt into remaining butter in saucepan; cook, stirring constantly, until mixture bubbles; stir in milk and mustard. Continue cooking and stirring until mixture thickens and bubbles 1 minute. Stir in 2 cups of the cheese until melted.
4. Pour sauce over spaghetti in saucepan and stir until well blended. Spoon half the spaghetti mixture into an 8-cup shallow baking dish; top with egg slices; add remaining spaghetti. Sprinkle remaining 1 cup cheese over top of casserole and top with buttered bread crumbs.
5. Bake in moderate oven (350°) 30 minutes, or until casserole bubbles and crumbs are golden. Makes 6 servings.

BAKED SPINACH AND EGGS AU GRATIN

- 2 cups bread cubes (6 slices)
- ½ cup (1 stick) butter or margarine
- 2 packages (10 ounces each) frozen chopped spinach
- 1 medium-size onion, chopped (½ cup)
- 1 cup cubed Muenster cheese
- 2 teaspoons salt
- ⅛ teaspoon pepper
- ⅛ teaspoon ground nutmeg
- ¼ cup flour
- 1 cup milk
- ⅓ cup grated Parmesan cheese
- 8 eggs

1. Sauté bread cubes in 2 tablespoons of the butter or margarine in medium-size skillet until golden; place in the bottom of a lightly greased 6-cup baking dish. Sauté onion until tender in same skillet in 2 more tablespoons butter or margarine; reserve.
2. Cook spinach, following label directions, in medium-size saucepan; drain very well. Return to saucepan; add onion, Muenster cheese, salt, pepper and nutmeg. Spoon over bread cubes in baking dish.
3. Melt remaining butter or margarine in a small saucepan; stir in flour; cook, stirring constantly, just until mixture bubbles. Stir in milk slowly; continue cooking and stirring until sauce thickens and bubbles 1 minute. Remove from heat.
4. Stir in Parmesan cheese. Let mixture cool.

5. Separate 4 of the eggs. Beat egg whites in a medium-size bowl just until they begin to form soft peaks.

6. Beat egg yolks in a large bowl until thick and fluffy; beat in cooled white sauce mixture, a small amount at a time. Carefully fold in egg whites until no streaks of white remain.

7. Make 4 indentations with a spoon in the spinach mixture, 1 inch from edge of dish. Carefully break remaining eggs, one in each indentation. Spoon soufflé mixture completely over the top, right to the edge.

8. Bake in moderate oven (325°) 45 minutes, or until puffy-firm and golden. Serve at once. Makes 4 servings.

CHEESE BLINTZES

Batter:
   5 eggs
   2 cups sifted all-purpose flour
2½ cups milk
   ⅓ cup vegetable oil
Cheese Filling:
   1 container (2 pounds) cream-style cottage cheese
   2 eggs
   ⅓ cup sugar
1½ teaspoons vanilla
   ⅓ cup butter or margarine
Topping:
   1 can (1 pound, 5 ounces) cherry pie filling
   2 cups (1-pint carton) dairy sour cream

1. To make Batter: Beat eggs just until blended in a large bowl; sift flour over the eggs and beat in just until smooth; stir in milk and oil. Cover; chill for at least 45 minutes. While batter chills, prepare filling.

2. To make Cheese Filling: Combine cottage cheese, eggs, sugar and vanilla in large bowl. Beat at high speed with electric beater 3 minutes, or until smooth.

3. Heat a heavy 8-inch skillet slowly; test temperature by sprinkling on a few drops of water. When drops bounce about, temperature is right. Grease skillet lightly with part of the butter.

4. Measure batter, a scant ¼ cup at a time, into skillet, tilting it to cover the bottom completely.

5. Cook blintz 1 to 2 minutes, or until top is set and underside is golden; remove to a plate. Repeat with remaining batter to make 24 blintzes.

Sandwich each blintz with a piece of foil or wax paper to keep separated.

6. Place 3 tablespoons of the cheese filling down the center of the golden side of each blintz. Overlap two opposite sides over filling, then fold up ends toward middle on seam side.

7. Melt remaining butter or margarine in a large skillet. Brown blintzes, seam side down, turning to brown on other side. Keep warm until all blintzes have been browned. Serve blintzes warm, topped with cherry pie filling and a dollop of sour cream. Makes 12 servings.

TRIPLE CHEESE SOUFFLÉ

1½ cups shredded cheese (6 ounces)
   6 tablespoons (¾ stick) butter or margarine
   ⅓ cup flour
   1 teaspoon salt
   1 teaspoon onion powder
1½ cups milk
   Few drops hot red-pepper seasoning
   3 eggs, separated

1. Prepare an ungreased 6-cup soufflé or straight-side baking dish this way: Fold a piece of foil, 28 inches long, in half lengthwise; wrap around dish to make a 3-inch stand-up collar; hold in place with string and a paper clip.

2. Use any combination of cheese you have in your refrigerator, to make the 1½ cups. (We used Cheddar, Muenster and Parmesan.)

3. Melt butter or margarine in a medium-size saucepan; stir in flour, salt and onion powder; cook, stirring constantly, until mixture bubbles 1 minute; stir in milk and red-pepper seasoning; continue cooking and stirring until mixture thickens and bubbles 1 minute; stir in grated cheeses until melted; let cool while beating eggs.

4. Beat egg whites till they form soft peaks in a large bowl.

5. Beat egg yolks well in small bowl; beat in cooled cheese sauce very slowly until well blended. Fold this mixture into beaten egg whites until no streaks of white or yellow remain. Pour into prepared dish; make a deep circle in center with knife so soufflé will puff up high.

6. Bake in a slow oven (325°) for 1 hour, 15 minutes, or until puffy-firm and golden. Serve at once. Makes 6 servings.

CHEESE & EGGS

CHEESE AND EGGPLANT CASSEROLE

        1 large eggplant (about 1½ pounds)
        3 tablespoons olive or vegetable oil
        1 large onion, chopped (1 cup)
    1 ½ cups soft white bread crumbs (3 slices)
        1 teaspoon salt
        1 teaspoon leaf oregano, crumbled
        ¼ teaspoon pepper
        1 container (1 pound) cottage cheese
        2 eggs
        ¼ cup chopped parsley
        ½ teaspoon salt
        2 medium-size tomatoes, sliced
        1 package (8 ounces) mozzarella cheese,
          sliced

1. Slice, pare and dice eggplant. Sauté in oil until soft; push to one side; sauté onion until soft; stir in bread crumbs, the 1 teaspoon salt, oregano and pepper; remove from heat.
2. Combine cottage cheese, eggs, parsley and the ½ teaspoon salt in a medium-size bowl.
3. Spoon half the eggplant mixture into an 8x8x2-inch baking dish; spread cottage cheese mixture over; top with remaining eggplant. Overlap slices of tomato over eggplant and top with slices of mozzarella cheese.
4. Bake in moderate oven (350°) 45 minutes; remove from oven and allow to set for 10 minutes before serving. Makes 6 servings.

PUFFY OMELET WITH CHEESE SAUCE

        4 tablespoons (½ stick) butter or margarine
        2 tablespoons flour
        ¾ teaspoon salt
        1 cup milk
        4 wedges process Gruyère cheese (from a 6-
          ounce package), shredded
        4 eggs, separated
        2 tablespoons water
          Dash of pepper
        1 tablespoon chopped green chili (from a 4-
          ounce can)

1. Make cheese sauce: Melt 2 tablespoons of the butter or margarine in a small saucepan; add flour and ½ teaspoon of the salt. Cook over low heat, stirring constantly, just until bubbly. Remove from heat; stir in milk slowly. Cook, stirring constantly, until sauce thickens and

bubbles 1 minute. Remove from heat; stir in cheese little by little until melted and smooth. Cover; keep warm while preparing remaining ingredients.
2. Beat egg whites until stiff in a large bowl.
3. Beat egg yolks with remaining ¼ teaspoon salt and pepper until thick and lemon-colored in a small bowl; beat in water. Fold into egg-white mixture until no streaks of yellow remain.
4. Heat a 9-inch skillet or omelet pan with an ovenproof handle, 5 seconds over medium heat. With a fork, swirl remaining 2 tablespoons butter or margarine over bottom and sides.
5. Pour in egg mixture. Cook over low heat 5 minutes, or until mixture is set on the bottom and is golden-brown.
6. Bake in moderate oven (350°) 10 minutes, or until puffy and lightly golden on the top.
7. Loosen omelet around edge with a knife; lift onto heated large serving plate. Cut a gash with a knife down center of omelet; sprinkle green chili over one half. Spoon about ¾ cup of the cheese sauce over omelet; fold over with spatula. Spoon remaining sauce over the top. Serve at once. Makes 2 servings.

TWO-CHEESE GNOCCHI

        5 cups water
        1 teaspoon salt
        1 cup enriched farina
        2 eggs, beaten
        1 cup shredded Swiss cheese
        ¼ teaspoon pepper
        ¼ cup (½ stick) butter or margarine
        1 cup grated Parmesan cheese

1. Heat water with salt to boiling in a large saucepan; sprinkle in farina and stir until well blended; lower heat and simmer 15 minutes.
2. Remove saucepan from heat and beat in eggs, Swiss cheese and pepper. Return saucepan to heat and cook, stirring constantly, until mixture thickens, about 3 minutes.
3. Pour mixture into a buttered 15x9x1-inch baking pan; chill 30 minutes, or until set.
4. Cut mixture into 1½-inch diamonds and arrange, overlapping, in an 8-cup baking dish.
5. Melt butter or margarine in a small saucepan; drizzle over; sprinkle cheese on top.
6. Bake in hot oven (400°) 30 minutes, or until tips of gnocchi are golden. Makes 4 servings.

8

COMPANY MEALS

Right from the beginning with our cover photograph of Hearty Cassoulet, we knew you'd have company on your mind. After all, a food budget that only allows for the same number of people night after night, just isn't realistic. We've designed this chapter with reality in mind, and the recipes are geared to those times when you have at least eight people to feed—eight people you want to entertain well, but economically. Of course, if you're only planning a dinner for four or six, almost any recipe in this book will work. Or, you can prepare these larger dinners and know you'll have plenty for second helpings or for leftovers to stash in the freezer for that time when unexpected guests arrive. Try our recipes. They'll help put economy on the company menu—and the only thing your guests will know is that you're a marvelous cook.

HEARTY CASSOULET

   1 package (1 pound) dried white Great North-
      ern beans
   8 cups water
   2 large onions, peeled
   6 whole cloves
   2 stalks celery, with tops
   3 sprigs parsley
   2 bay leaves
      Salt
   ½ pound salt pork, cut in ½-inch cubes
   1 pound lean breast of lamb, cut in 1½-inch
      pieces
   1 carrot, sliced
   2 cloves garlic, crushed
   1 can (6 ounces) tomato paste
   2 cups water
   2 envelopes or teaspoons instant chicken
      broth
   1 teaspoon leaf thyme
   4 pork chops (about 1¼ pounds)
   ½ pound pork sausage, shaped into 8 small
      patties

1. Place beans in a kettle; add 8 cups water;
heat to boiling; cover. Cook 2 minutes; remove
from heat; let stand 1 hour. Stud one of the
onions with cloves, add to beans along with
tops from celery, the parsley and bay leaves tied
together with string; stir in 1 teaspoon salt; bring
to boiling. Reduce heat and simmer, covered, 1
to 1½ hours, or until beans are tender. Drain,
reserving liquid. Remove and discard parsley
bundle.
2. Meanwhile, sauté salt pork until crisp in
Dutch oven; remove and set aside. Pour off
drippings; return 2 tablespoons to pan.
3. Brown lamb in hot drippings; remove and set
aside. Slice remaining onion and celery stalks;
add to drippings along with carrot and garlic;
saute until golden, about 8 minutes. Return lamb
and pork to Dutch oven. Stir in tomato paste, 2
cups water, instant chicken broth, thyme and 1
teaspoon salt; bring to boiling. Simmer, covered,
1 hour.
4. Add the beans and ½ cup of bean liquid to
lamb mixture; adjust seasonings if needed. Turn
into a 3-quart casserole.
5. Brown pork chops on both sides in a large
skillet; add to bean mixture. Brown pork sausage patties in same skillet; set aside.
6. Bake in moderate oven (350°) 30 minutes.

Carefully stir beans, adding more bean liquid if
too dry. Arrange sausage patties on top. Bake 30
minutes longer. Makes 8 servings.

CURRIED LAMB WITH GOLDEN PILAF

   4 pounds lamb combination (neck and
      shoulder meat for stewing)
   2 cups water
   2 tablespoons vegetable oil
   3 cups cooking apples, pared, quartered,
      cored and chopped
   1 cup chopped celery
   5 teaspoons curry powder
   2 teaspoons salt
      Golden Pilaf (recipe follows)

1. Cut meat from bones of lamb combination;
cut meat into 1-inch pieces.
2. Place bones and water in a medium-size
saucepan. Heat to boiling; reduce heat; cover.
Simmer 30 minutes. Strain broth into a 2-cup
measure (you should have 1½ cups); reserve.
3. Brown lamb pieces slowly, part at a time, in
oil in a large skillet with a cover; remove meat
with a slotted spoon and reserve.
4. Stir apple and celery into drippings in skillet;
saute until soft; blend in curry powder and
cook 1 minute. Stir in reserved lamb broth and
salt. Heat to boiling; reduce heat; cover. Simmer 10 minutes. Mash this mixture with the
back of a wooden spoon to make a smoother
sauce.
5. Return reserved meat to skillet; cover; simmer 1 hour, or until meat is tender. Serve with
Golden Pilaf. Makes 8 servings.

GOLDEN PILAF

   2 cups uncooked regular rice
   ¼ cup vegetable oil
   1 large onion, chopped (1 cup)
   2 envelopes instant chicken broth or 2 tea-
      spoons granulated chicken bouillon
   2 teaspoons salt
   5 cups hot water
   ½ cup golden raisins

1. Sauté rice, stirring often, in oil until golden-
brown in a large skillet; remove with spoon.

2. Sauté onion until soft in oil remaining in same pan; return rice to skillet with onion, chicken broth, salt, hot water and raisins.

3. Heat to boiling; reduce heat to low; cover. Simmer 35 minutes, or until liquid is absorbed and rice is tender. Makes 8 servings.

SPINACH LASAGNA

    1   pound ground beef
    ½   pound sweet Italian sausages
    2   large onions, chopped (2 cups)
    1   clove of garlic, minced
    1   can (2 pounds, 3 ounces) Italian tomatoes
        with tomato paste
    3   teaspoons salt
    2   teaspoons Italian herbs, crumbled
    ¼   teaspoon pepper
    1   package (1 pound) lasagna noodles
    2   eggs
    2   packages (10 ounces each) frozen chopped
        spinach, thawed and drained well
    1   carton (1 pound) cottage cheese
    1   cup grated Parmesan cheese
    2   packages (6 ounces each) sliced mozzarella
        cheese

1. Brown ground beef and Italian sausages in a large kettle; remove with a slotted spoon; reserve. Pour off all but 3 tablespoons of the fat. Saute onion and garlic until soft in fat in kettle. Return browned meat to kettle with Italian tomatoes, 2 teaspoons of the salt, Italian herbs and pepper. Simmer over low heat, stirring several times, 30 minutes.

2. While sauce simmers: Cook lasagna noodles, following label directions; drain and place in a bowl of cold water to keep separated.

3. Beat eggs in a large bowl; add drained spinach, cottage cheese and remaining 1 teaspoon of the salt.

4. When ready to assemble: Drain noodles on paper toweling; arrange 3 strips on the bottom of each of two 13x9x2-inch baking dishes. Spoon part of the cheese-spinach mixture over noodles; add part of meat sauce; sprinkle with grated Parmesan cheese. Continue layering until all ingredients have been used. Top each dish with slices of mozzarella cheese.

5. Bake in moderate oven (350°) 30 minutes, or until bubbly-hot. Garnish with sprigs of parsley, if you wish. Makes 12 servings.

NOTE: These dishes can be made early in the day. Assemble lasagna and keep in the refrigerator until 1 hour before party time. Place in cold oven and turn heat to 350°. Bake 1 hour, or until bubbly-hot.

ALGERIAN COUSCOUS

    2   large onions, chopped (2 cups)
    2   tablespoons olive oil
    1   broiler-fryer (about 2½ pounds), cut up
    1   pound lean lamb, cut into 1½-inch cubes
    3   cups water
    4   carrots, pared and cut into 1-inch pieces
    3   teaspoons salt
    ¼   teaspoon pepper
    ¼   teaspoon ground ginger
    1   three-inch piece stick cinnamon
    1   teaspoon salt (for couscous)
    1   cup water (for couscous)
    1   package (1 pound, 1¾ ounces) couscous*
        (2¾ cups)
    4   small zucchini, washed and cut into ½-inch
        slices
    2   fresh tomatoes, chopped
    1   can (1 pound, 4 ounces) chick peas, drained
    1   cup seedless raisins
    6   tablespoons (¾ stick) butter or margarine,
        melted

1. Sauté onions until golden in oil in a large skillet, about 5 minutes. Transfer to a stock pot or similar deep narrow kettle. Brown chicken and lamb in same skillet; transfer to stock pot as it browns.

2. Add water to skillet; bring to boiling, scraping off brown bits. Pour over meat. Stir in carrots, salt, pepper, ginger and cinnamon. Bring to boiling.

3. For couscous, dissolve salt in 1 cup water; sprinkle about ½ cup over couscous in a large bowl to moisten; place in a large, fine-mesh sieve. Hang sieve on edge of stock pot over stew, making sure the sieve does not touch stew. Cover tightly with foil to keep steam in. Simmer 40 minutes.

4. Remove sieve; stir zucchini, tomatoes, chick peas and raisins into stew. Sprinkle remaining salted water over couscous; mix or stir with a fork. Set sieve over stew again to steam. Simmer 30 minutes longer, or until meats and vegetables are tender. Thicken stew with a little flour mixed

with water, if you wish. Turn couscous into a large bowl; drizzle melted butter or margarine over; toss to mix.

5. To serve, spoon stew into center of a deep platter. Arrange the steamed buttered couscous around edge. Makes 8 servings.

*You may substitute brown or white rice or kasha and cook, following label directions.

GREEK LAMB STEW, AVGOLEMONO
(Lamb and Artichoke Stew)

    3 pounds lean lamb, cut into 1½-inch cubes
    2 tablespoons olive or vegetable oil
    1 large onion, sliced
    ½ cup dry white wine
    2 cups water
    2 teaspoons salt
    ⅛ teaspoon pepper
    1 bay leaf
    1 tablespoon chopped fresh dill
      OR: 1 teaspoon dried dill weed
    2 packages (9 ounces each) frozen artichoke hearts
    2 tablespoons flour
    ¼ cup dry white wine
    3 eggs
    ¼ cup fresh lemon juice

1. Brown lamb, part at a time (removing pieces to a bowl as they brown), in oil in heavy kettle or Dutch oven. Add onion; sauté until golden, about 5 minutes. Return meat to kettle. Add ½ cup wine; lower heat; cover. Simmer about 15 minutes.

2. Stir in water, salt, pepper and bay leaf. Simmer, covered, over low heat, 1 hour and 15 minutes, or until meat is tender.

3. Add dill and artichokes. Cook 10 minutes longer, or until artichokes are tender.

4. Remove bay leaf. Then remove meat and artichokes from cooking liquid with slotted spoon; arrange in a shallow serving casserole. Cover and keep hot while making sauce. Measure cooking liquid, there should be about 3 cups; add wine or water, if needed. Bring to boiling.

5. Blend flour and ¼ cup wine in a small cup; stir into boiling liquid. Cook and stir until sauce thickens and bubbles 1 minute.

6. Beat eggs with rotary beater or electric hand mixer until light and fluffy; beat in lemon juice. Gradually beat boiling sauce into egg mixture.

Return to saucepan; heat, stirring constantly, over low heat, 1 minute. (Sauce should not boil.)

7. To serve, pour sauce over meat and artichokes in casserole. Garnish casserole with lemon slices and sprigs of fresh dill, if you wish. (See photograph at bottom far right on page 95.) Makes 8 servings.

TWIN-MEAT RAGOUT

    3 pounds lean boneless lamb shoulder, cut in 1-inch cubes
    3 pounds veal shoulder, cut into cubes, about 1 inch each
    2 large onions, peeled and sliced thin
    1 large head iceberg lettuce, shredded
    3 teaspoons salt
    ¼ teaspoon pepper
    1½ teaspoons leaf rosemary, crumbled
    5 envelopes instant chicken broth or 5 teaspoons granulated chicken bouillon
      Water
    16 medium-size potatoes, pared
    1 bag (2 pounds) frozen peas
    4 medium-size yellow squashes, sliced
    2 cups (1 pint) cherry tomatoes
    1 tablespoon butter or margarine
    ¼ cup cornstarch

1. Combine lamb and veal with onions, lettuce, salt, pepper and rosemary in a large roasting pan. Sprinkle chicken broth or bouillon over top; pour 6 cups water into pan. Heat to boiling; cover. Simmer 1 hour. Place potatoes on top; simmer 1 hour longer, or until meats and potatoes are tender.

2. About 15 minutes before meats are cooked, cook peas and squashes in boiling salted water in separate medium-size saucepans just until crisply tender; drain.

3. Sauté tomatoes in butter or margarine in a medium-size frying pan, shaking pan often, 3 minutes, or just until hot.

4. Smooth cornstarch and about ½ cup water to a paste in a cup; stir into stew mixture. Cook, stirring constantly, until mixture thickens and boils 3 minutes.

5. Spoon stew mixture into two heated large serving dishes; spoon squash slices, then peas, in rings on top of each. Pile tomatoes in center. Garnish each tomato with a sprig of fresh rosemary, if you wish. Makes 16 servings.

Top right: Algerian Couscous, a lamb and chicken stew from the Middle East. Bottom, from left to right: Texas Chili Beef Stew and Greek Lamb Stew. The recipes for all three are in this chapter.

COMPANY MEALS

GLAZED PORK SHOULDER

- 1 cook-before-eating smoked pork picnic shoulder (about 5 pounds)
  Water
- 1 tablespoon mixed pickling spices
- 1 cup firmly packed brown sugar
- 1 cup apple juice
- ¼ teaspoon ground cloves
- ½ cup chopped parsley

1. Place picnic shoulder in a kettle; add cold water to cover; add pickling spices.
2. Heat slowly to boiling; reduce heat; cover. Simmer 2½ hours, or until meat is tender when pierced with a two-tined fork. Remove from heat; allow meat to cool in liquid at least 30 minutes.
3. Place picnic shoulder in a shallow roasting pan. Cut skin from top of meat; score fat.
4. To make Parsley Sauce: Combine brown sugar, apple juice and cloves in a small saucepan. Heat to boiling; reduce heat; simmer 5 minutes. Remove sauce from heat; stir in chopped parsley. Brush part of sauce over meat.
5. Roast in moderate oven (375°), basting several times with part of sauce, 30 minutes, or until well-glazed.
6. Pass remaining Parsley Sauce separately. Serve with baked sweet potatoes and spiced pear halves, if you wish. Makes 12 servings.

BAKED OXTAIL RAGOUT

- 4 pounds oxtails
- ½ cup flour
- 1 teaspoon salt
- 1 teaspoon leaf savory, crumbled
- ¼ teaspoon pepper
- ¼ cup vegetable oil
- 1 large onion, chopped (1 cup)
- 1 can (12 ounces) carrot juice
- 1½ cups water
- ½ cup dry red wine
- 1 bay leaf

1. Cut oxtails into uniform length pieces.
2. Shake pieces in a mixture of flour, salt, savory and pepper in a plastic bag to coat well; reserve remaining seasoned flour for use in Step 4 (you should have about 2 tablespoons).
3. Brown pieces slowly, part at a time, in oil in a large skillet; remove pieces with a slotted spoon to an 8-cup baking dish.
4. Stir onion into drippings in skillet; sauté until soft. Stir in reserved seasoned flour; cook, stirring, just until bubbly. Stir in carrot juice, water and wine; continue cooking and stirring, until gravy thickens and bubbles 1 minute. Pour over meat in baking dish; add bay leaf; cover.
5. Bake in moderate oven (375°) 2 hours, or until meat separates easily from bones.
6. Ladle ragout into soap plates; serve with French bread, if you wish. Makes 8 servings.

TEXAS CHILI BEEF STEW

- 4 pounds beef short ribs
- 1 large onion, chopped (1 cup)
- 1 green pepper, halved, seeded and diced
- 2 cloves garlic, chopped
- 2 tablespoons chili powder
- 1 can (1 pound) tomatoes
- 1 can (4 ounces) green chilies, drained and chopped
- 1 envelope or teaspoon instant beef broth
- 1 cup boiling water
- 1 teaspoon salt
- 2 tablespoons flour
- ¼ cup water
- 2 cans (1 pound each) kidney beans, drained
- 1 can (1 pound) whole kernel corn, drained

1. Heat heavy kettle or Dutch oven; rub fat edges of short ribs over bottom until about 2 tablespoons of fat melt. Brown short ribs well on all sides; remove. Drain off fat.
2. Sauté onion, green pepper and garlic in same pan. Stir in chili powder; cook, stirring constantly, about 2 minutes. Add tomatoes and green chilies. Dissolve instant beef broth in boiling water; stir into tomato mixture. Return ribs to pan. Bring to boiling; lower heat; cover. Simmer 2 hours, or until meat is very tender and falls away from the bones.
3. Remove meat to serving bowl; keep warm. Carefully remove bones and skim fat from sauce in pan. Blend flour and water in a cup; mix well. Stir into sauce. Cook, stirring constantly, until sauce bubbles and thickens. Add kidney beans and corn; heat about 5 minutes. Spoon over meat in serving bowl. Makes 8 servings.

9

SOUPS 'N' STEWS

Slow-simmered soups and stews are two great ways to expand your menu and still trim the food budget. They're not difficult to prepare either, as the recipes in this chapter prove. Here you'll find ideas for one-pot seafood, meat, poultry and vegetable combinations, some made from scratch, others made with convenience-oriented foods that are perfect for busy nights. The Basic Beef Broth and Basic Chicken Broth recipes also offer you make-ahead flexibility. Then, as dinnertime rolls around, add leftover meats and vegetables or use the broths as the basis for a delicious onion soup, a chicken and vegetable stew or a stick-to-the-ribs beef and vegetable soup. The cost? Some of these specials can be made for a very small cost. Others, though a bit more expensive, still provide your money's worth in flavor, nutrition and number of servings.

ONION SOUP

    4 large onions, sliced (1½ pounds)
    4 tablespoons (½ stick) butter or margarine
    6 cups Basic Beef Broth (see below)
    2 teaspoons salt
    ¼ teaspoon pepper
    6 slices French bread, toasted
    ½ cup grated Parmesan cheese
    ¼ cup Gruyere or Swiss cheese

1. Saute onion in butter or margarine in Dutch oven 15 minutes, or until lightly browned. Stir in Beef Broth, salt and pepper. Bring to boiling; reduce heat; cover; simmer 30 minutes.
2. Ladle soup into 6 ovenproof soup bowls or 12-ounce custard cups, or an 8-cup casserole. Lay bread slices on top, sprinkle with cheeses.
3. Heat in very hot oven (425°) 10 minutes, then place under preheated broiler and broil until top is bubbly and lightly browned. Makes 6 servings.

BASIC BEEF BROTH

  2½ pounds brisket, boneless chuck, or bottom
       round, in one piece
    2 pounds shin of beef with bones
    2 three-inch marrow bones
    1 veal knuckle (about 1 pound)
       Water
    8 teaspoons salt
    2 carrots, pared
    2 medium-size yellow onions, peeled
    2 stalks celery with leaves
    1 turnip, pared and quartered
    1 leek, washed well
    3 large sprigs of parsley
   12 peppercorns
    3 whole cloves
    1 bay leaf

1. Place beef, shin of beef, marrow bones and veal knuckle in a large kettle; add water to cover, about 4 quarts. Heat to boiling; skim off foam that appears on top. Add salt, carrots, onions, celery, turnip and leek; tie parsley, peppercorns, cloves and bay leaf in a small cheesecloth bag; add to kettle. Push under the liquid and add more water if needed.
2. Heat to boiling; cover; reduce heat; simmer very slowly 3½ to 4 hours, or until meat is tender. Remove meat and vegetables from broth.
3. Strain broth through cheesecloth into a large bowl. (There should be about 14 cups.) Use this broth in making Onion Soup (see left) or in any of our recipes calling for beef broth.
4. When meat is cool enough to handle, remove and dicard bones. Trim large piece of meat and save for another meal, if you wish. Cut trimmings and shin beef into bite-size pieces; serve as is, or use as the basic stock in Old-Fashioned Beef and Vegetable Soup (see page 99). To store in refrigerator up to 3 to 4 days, keep in covered container. To freeze, pack in small portions, 1 or 2 cups, in plastic bags or freezer containers, to use as needed.
5. To store in refrigerator, up to 4 days, leave fat layer on surface of broth until ready to use, then lift off and discard before heating. To freeze: Transfer broth to freezer containers, allowing space on top for expansion; freeze until ready to use (3 to 4 months maximum.) Makes 14 cups.

BASIC CHICKEN BROTH

    2 broiler-fryers, 3 to 3½ pounds each
       Chicken giblets
    2 medium carrots, pared
    1 large parsnip, pared
    1 large onion, chopped (1 cup)
    2 stalks celery
    2 celery tops
    3 sprigs parsley
    1 leek, washed well
       Water
    2 tablespoons salt
   12 peppercorns

1. Combine chicken, chicken giblets, carrots, parsnip, onion and celery in a large kettle; tie celery tops, parsley and leek together with a string; add to kettle. Add enough cold water to cover chicken and vegetables, about 12 cups.
2. Heat slowly to boiling; skim; add salt and peppercorns; reduce heat. Simmer very slowly 1 to 1½ hours, or until meat falls off the bones. Remove meat and vegetables from broth, discard the bundle of greens.
3. Strain broth through cheesecloth into a large bowl. (There should be about 12 cups.) Use this broth in the recipe for Mulligatawny Soup.
4. When cool enough to handle, remove and

discard skin and bones from chicken; cut meat into bite-size pieces; use as called for in following recipes, or use in salads, casseroles, etc. To store in refrigerator, up to 3 to 4 days, keep in covered container. To freeze, pack in small portions, 1 or 2 cups, in plastic bags or freezer containers, to use as needed.

5. To store in refrigerator, up to 4 days, leave fat layer on surface of broth until ready to use, then lift fat off and discard, or use in other cooking. To freeze, transfer broth to freezer containers, allowing space on top for expansion. Freeze until ready to use (3 to 4 months maximum). Makes 12 cups or enough for 2 soups, and even extra meat for a salad or casserole, if you wish.

MULLIGATAWNY SOUP

    3 medium carrots, pared and sliced
    2 stalks of celery, sliced
    6 cups Basic Chicken Broth (see page 98)
    3 cups cooked diced chicken (from Basic Chicken Broth)
    1 large onion, chopped (1 cup)
    4 tablespoons (½ stick) butter or margarine
    1 apple, pared, quartered, cored and chopped
    5 teaspoons curry powder
    1 teaspoon salt
    ¼ cup flour
    1 tablespoon lemon juice
    2 cups hot cooked rice
    ¼ cup chopped parsley
    6 lemon slices (optional)

1. Cook carrots and celery in 1 cup broth in a medium-size saucepan 20 minutes, or until tender. Add chicken; heat just until hot; cover; keep warm.
2. Saute onion until soft in butter or margarine in Dutch oven; stir in apple, curry powder and salt; saute 5 minutes longer, or until apple is soft; add flour. Gradually stir in remaining chicken broth; heat to boiling, stirring constantly; reduce heat; cover; simmer 15 minutes.
3. Add vegetables and chicken with the broth they were cooked in; bring just to boiling. Stir in lemon juice.
4. Ladle into soup plates or bowls; pass hot cooked rice and chopped parsley and lemon slices, if you wish, for each to add his own. Good with French bread. Makes 6 servings.

OLD-FASHIONED BEEF AND VEGETABLE SOUP

    1½ quarts Basic Beef Broth (see page 98)
    2 potatoes, peeled and diced (2 cups)
    2 carrots, pared and sliced
    1 cup sliced celery
    2 small onions, peeled and quartered
    1 can (1 pound) whole tomatoes
    2 teaspoons salt
    ⅛ teaspoon pepper
    ½ head green cabbage, shredded (2 cups)
    1 cup frozen corn (from a plastic bag)
    3 cups diced boiled beef (from Basic Beef Broth)
    1 tablespoon chopped parsley

1. Heat Beef Broth to boiling in a large saucepan or kettle; add potatoes, carrots, celery, onions, tomatoes, salt and pepper; heat to boiling again; lower heat; cover; simmer for 20 minutes.
2. Stir in cabbage, corn and meat; simmer 10 minutes longer or just until all vegetables are crisply tender. Sprinkle with parsley.
3. Ladle into soup bowls. Makes 8 servings.

BLACK BEAN SOUP

    4 cups dried black turtle beans (from two 1-pound bags)
    3½ quarts water
    ½ pound pepperoni, cut into ½-inch pieces
    3 large onions, sliced (3 cups)
    1 boneless smoked pork butt (about 2 pounds)
    2 cups dry red wine
    3 oranges, peeled and sectioned
    2 teaspoons salt
    ¼ cup chopped parsley

1. Combine beans with water in a large kettle; heat to boiling and boil 2 minutes; cover. Remove from heat; let stand 1 hour.
2. Heat beans to boiling again; add pepperoni and onions; reduce heat; cover. Simmer 2 hours, stirring occasionally, or until beans are tender. Add pork and wine. Simmer 1¼ hours longer, or until meat is cooked through.
3. Remove meat and keep warm. With a slotted spoon, remove pieces of sausage and about 3 cups of whole beans. Puree remaining beans in soup in a blender or press them through sieve.

Return beans to kettle along with sausage and the whole beans.

4. Add sections from 2 of the oranges and salt. Taste; add additional salt, if you wish. Bring to boiling; ladle into soup bowls. Garnish each serving with a section of reserved orange; sprinkle with parsley.

5. Slice pork butt thin and pass it around to eat, on a separate plate, with mustard and bread. Makes 12 servings.

NOTE: This dish can easily be made ahead of time because it freezes well. (Freeze soup and meats separately, sealing both in refrigerator-freezer containers.)

CIOPPINO

        1 large onion, chopped (1 cup)
        1 medium-size green pepper, halved, seeded and chopped
      ½ cup sliced celery
        1 carrot, pared and shredded
        3 cloves of garlic, minced
        3 tablespoons olive oil
        2 cans (1 pound each) tomatoes
        1 can (8 ounces) tomato sauce
        1 teaspoon leaf basil, crumbled
        1 bay leaf
        1 teaspoon salt
      ¼ teaspoon pepper
        1 pound frozen halibut or turbot
        1 dozen mussels in shell, if available
           OR: 1 can (10 ounces) clams in shell
   1½ cups dry white wine
        1 package (8 ounces) frozen, shelled, deveined shrimp
      ½ pound fresh or frozen scallops
        2 tablespoons minced parsley

1. Sauté onion, green pepper, celery, carrot and garlic in olive oil until soft in a kettle or Dutch oven.

2. Stir in tomatoes, tomato sauce, basil, bay leaf, salt and pepper; heat to boiling; lower heat; cover; simmer 2 hours. Discard bay leaf.

3. While sauce simmers, remove the skin from the halibut or turbot; cut into serving-size pieces. Using a stiff brush, thoroughly scrub the mussels, cutting off their "beards," under running water to remove any residue of mud and sand. Reserve for use in Step 5.

4. Stir wine into sauce in kettle. Add the fish, shrimp and scallops. Simmer, covered, 10 minutes longer.

5. Place mussels or clams in a layer on top of fish in kettle; cover; steam 5 to 10 minutes, or until the shells are fully opened and fish flakes easily. (Discard any unopened mussels.)

6. Ladle into soup plates or bowls. Sprinkle with parsley. Serve with sourdough bread, or crusty French or Italian bread. Makes 8 servings.

NOTE: If fresh clams are available and reasonably priced, use 1 dozen in place of the canned clams. Be sure to rinse them well before adding to soup, and discard any that do not open once they have been cooked.

BOOTHBAY CHOWDER

        3 slices bacon, chopped
        1 large onion, chopped (1 cup)
        4 medium-size potatoes, pared and diced (3 cups)
        3 cups water
        1 teaspoon salt
      ¼ teaspoon pepper
        2 cans (10½ ounces each) minced clams
        1 bottle (8 ounces) clam juice
        1 envelope instant nonfat dry milk (for 1 quart)
        3 tablespoons flour
        2 tablespoons minced parsley

1. Cook bacon until crisp in a large heavy saucepan or Dutch oven. Remove bacon with slotted spoon; drain on paper toweling; reserve. Add onion to bacon drippings in saucepan; sauté until soft.

2. Add potatoes, 2 cups of the water, salt and pepper; cover. Simmer, 15 minutes, or until potatoes are tender. Remove from heat.

3. Drain liquid from clams into a 4-cup measure; reserve clams. Add bottled clam juice and remaining cup of water.

4. Combine dry milk with flour in a small bowl; stir briskly into clam liquids in cup. Add to potato mixture in saucepan. Cook, stirring constantly, over medium heat, until chowder thickens and bubbles 1 minute.

5. Add clams; heat just until piping-hot. Ladle into soup bowls. Sprinkle with parsley and reserved bacon. Serve with pilot crackers, if you wish. Makes 6 to 8 servings.

Right: Cioppino, a colorful, delicious soup-stew brimming with good food from the sea. It's delicious served with crusty bread.

HUNGARIAN PORK GOULASH

- 2 pounds pork, cut in 1-inch cubes
- 2 tablespoons butter or margarine
- 1 large onion, chopped (1 cup)
- 1 tablespoon paprika
- 1 can condensed chicken broth
- 1 cup water
- 1 teaspoon caraway seeds
- 2 teaspoons salt
- Dash of pepper
- 1 can (1 pound, 11 ounces) sauerkraut
- 2 tablespoons flour
- ¼ cup water
- 1 cup dairy sour cream
- Chopped parsley

1. Brown pork, part at a time (removing pieces to a bowl as they brown), in butter or margarine in a heavy kettle or Dutch oven. Sauté onion until golden, about 5 minutes, in same pan, adding more butter or margarine, if needed. Stir in paprika; cook 1 minute longer. Return meat.
2. Stir in chicken broth, 1 cup water, caraway seeds, salt and pepper. Heat to boiling; lower heat; cover. Simmer 1 hour and 15 minutes.
3. Drain and rinse sauerkraut; stir into stew. Simmer 30 minutes longer, or until tender.
4. Blend flour and ½ cup water in a small cup; stir into simmering stew. Cook and stir until gravy thickens and boils.
5. Lower heat; stir in sour cream, a tablespoon at a time, to prevent curdling. Heat just until heated through. Do not boil. Sprinkle with parsley. Makes 6 servings.

PETITE MARMITE

- Turkey carcass with meat
- Giblets (from freezer) (see Braised Turkey Persillade, page 36)
- 1 pound beef, brisket or flanken
- 8 cups cold water
- 1 large onion, studded with 2 cloves
- 1 small parsnip, pared and quartered
- 4 carrots
- 1 stalk celery with leaves, chopped
- 4 sprigs parsley
- 1 large leek (white part only)
- 2 stalks celery
- 1 white turnip
- 2 teaspoons salt
- ¼ teaspoon freshly ground pepper
- 2 cups Sauce (from Braised Turkey Persillade, page 36)

1. Cut any large pieces of meat still on turkey and reserve; remove all skin from carcass and break into as small pieces as possible.
2. Place turkey carcass in deep kettle; add frozen giblets, beef and water.
3. Heat to boiling; lower heat; simmer, skimming foam from surface, until liquid is clear. Add onion, quartered parsnip and 1 of the carrots, chopped celery with leaves, and parsley.
4. Simmer 1½ hours, or until beef is tender; remove kettle from heat and allow to stand until beef is cool enough to handle.
5. Cut beef into tiny cubes; cut off all remaining turkey from carcass; dice giblets. Strain soup into a large bowl; allow to cool until all fat has floated to the top; skim off all fat. Rinse kettle and return liquid to kettle with cut-up meats.
6. Slice leek; cut remaining 3 carrots and 2 stalks celery into julienne strips and dice turnip; add to kettle with salt, pepper and sauce from Braised Turkey Persillade.
7. Heat soup to boiling; lower heat; cook 1 hour, or until vegetables are very tender. Taste; add additional salt and pepper, if you wish. Ladle into heated soup bowls. Makes 8 servings.

GREEK LAMB STEW

- 2½ pounds lamb shoulder, cubed
- ¼ cup vegetable oil
- 3 medium-size onions, chopped (1½ cups)
- 1 clove garlic, minced
- 1 can (1 pound, 12 ounces) tomatoes
- 1 can (8 ounces) tomato sauce
- 1 cup water
- 2 teaspoons salt
- ½ teaspoon ground marjoram
- ¼ teaspoon ground pepper
- 1 small eggplant, peeled and cubed
- 1 large green pepper, seeded and cubed
- 1 cup uncooked elbow macaroni (from a 1-pound package)

1. Brown meat lightly in oil in a Dutch oven. Remove cubes; add garlic and onions; sauté 5 minutes, or until soft.
2. Add lamb cubes, tomatoes, tomato sauce,

Shown on pages 102-103: Boothbay Chowder, a robust meal-in-one made with seafood. Opposite: Another hearty main-dish soup, Old-Fashioned Beef and Vegetable Soup. Recipes for both soups are included in this chapter.

105

water, salt, marjoram and pepper; bring to boiling; lower heat and simmer, covered, 1 hour. Add eggplant, green pepper and macaroni; cook 30 minutes longer, or until meat and macaroni are tender. Makes 8 servings.

JAMBALAYA

2 broiler-fryers, about 2 pounds each, cut up
1 cup diced cooked ham
4 tablespoons (½ stick) butter or margarine
2 cloves garlic, minced
2 large onions, chopped (2 cups)
2 cans (1 pound each) stewed tomatoes
2 teaspoons salt
½ teaspoon chili powder
1 cup uncooked rice
2 cups sliced celery

1. Brown chicken pieces lightly in butter or margarine in Dutch oven. Remove chicken pieces; brown ham lightly. Add garlic and onions; saute 5 minutes, or until soft. Return chicken.
2. Add stewed tomatoes, salt and chili powder to chicken mixture; bring to boiling; lower heat; simmer, covered, 30 minutes. Add rice and celery; cook 30 minutes longer, or until chicken and rice are tender. Makes 8 servings.

UKRAINIAN KETTLE

1 bottom round beef roast (about 4 pounds)
2 tablespoons vegetable oil
1 large onion, diced (1 cup)
2 teaspoons seasoned salt
1 teaspoon seasoned pepper
1 can condensed beef broth
2 small yellow turnips (about 2½ pounds)
1 cup sliced celery

1. Brown meat on all sides in oil in a kettle or Dutch oven. Add onion, seasoned salt and pepper, and beef broth. Heat to boiling; reduce heat; cover. Simmer 2 hours.
2. Pare turnips; cut into 1-inch cubes. Add with celery to meat, turning to coat with liquid in kettle. Cover; simmer 1 hour longer, or until meat and vegetables are tender.
3. Place pot roast on a carving board; cut into thick slices; arrange on a platter. Remove vegetables from kettle with a slotted spoon and arrange around meat. Spoon cooking liquid over all. Or, use cooking liquid to prepare a gravy (recipe follows). Makes 8 servings.
GRAVY: Pour cooking liquid into a 2-cup measure; add water, if needed, to make 2 cups; return to kettle and bring to boiling. Blend ¼ cup flour with ¼ cup water in a jar with a tight-fitting lid; shake to mix well; stir into boiling liquid. Cook, stirring constantly, until gravy thickens and bubbles 1 minute. Pour a little gravy over the meat and serve the remainder separately.

COPENHAGEN OXTAIL SOUP

3 pounds oxtails, cut up
3 teaspoons salt
⅛ teaspoon pepper
1 large onion, chopped (1 cup)
2 carrots, pared and sliced (1 cup)
1 parsnip, pared and sliced (¾ cup)
1 turnip, pared and sliced (1 cup)
2 tablespoons brandy
6 cups water
½ teaspoon leaf savory, crumbled
1 bay leaf
Eggs Mimosa (recipe follows)
Chopped parsley

1. Spread oxtails in a single layer in shallow roasting pan. Season with salt and pepper. Roast in very hot oven (450°) 45 minutes, or until browned. Drain off fat, reserving 2 tablespoons.
2. Sauté onion, carrots, parsnip and turnip in reserved fat in kettle or Dutch oven, 10 minutes, or until soft. Add browned oxtails. Drizzle brandy over, ignite carefully with a lighted match. Add water to roasting pan in which oxtails were browned. Heat, stirring constantly, to dissolve browned bits; pour over oxtails and vegetables in Dutch oven; add savory and bay leaf. Bring to boiling; reduce heat; cover; simmer slowly 2 hours, or until meat separates easily from bones.
3. Ladle into soup bowls; place a half egg in each, sprinkle with parsley. Serve with crusty French bread. Makes 6 servings.
EGGS MIMOSA—Cut 3 hard-cooked eggs in half lengthwise. Carefully remove yolks, keeping whites whole. Press yolks through a sieve, spoon back into whites.

10
DINNER
SALADS & SANDWICHES

Serve lunch for dinner! Classically enjoyed as lunchtime fare or as an accompaniment to dinner, salads and sandwiches can be your dinner when a few extra touches are added. Our recipe for Salad Niçoise is a case in point. Starting with the basic greens and dressing, we added meat and cheese and turned this salad into a beautiful meal-in-one . . . for a low cost per serving. Then there's Bavarian Baked Potato Salad, a hot version of potato salad that includes frankfurters and cheese, and offers an even bigger budget break. The recipe makes enough for six people, at a reasonable price. For sandwich-style dinners we offer Steak-Medallions, Hot Tuna Heroes, Grilled Cheese for a Crowd, and many more. You'll find they're all geared to budget-watching but none scrimp on nutrition or inspiration. So have some lunch for dinner tonight!

SALADS & SANDWICHES: EATING BETTER, SPENDING LESS

• Don't wash away savings. For longer-lasting, fresher-tasting salad greens, don't wash them until you're ready to use them. Tomatoes and cucumbers get moldy and rot. Lettuce turns rusty and gets limp. Take only as much lettuce as you're going to need for your salad. Then wash and dry it, so dressings will cling to the leaves.

• For a change of pace in salads, along with a vitamin A boost, use escarole, chicory and spinach instead of iceberg lettuce. As another lettuce-and-tomatoes alternative, consider making your own coleslaw. Cabbage is reasonably priced and goes a long way. Use half for coleslaw, half for cooked cabbage and several outer leaves for rolled cabbage dinner.

• For further salad variety, look for the less familiar regional or seasonal greens. A few examples are: Prize head lettuce with red-edged leaves; lamb's lettuce; fennel, or finochio, with its distinctive anise flavor; the tender young dandelion, mustard and beet greens, plus Swiss chard. You can cook these greens, of course, but don't miss out on the unusual flavor touches that just a few, chopped up, will add to a salad.

• Save on salad dressings by making your own.

• Save on mayonnaise and salad dressing by buying the quart size. It's thriftier than two pints, even for the small family. Buy when your favorite brand is on sale—you may save as much as 10 to 20¢ a quart.

• Pick out fairly firm, medium-size heads of lettuce, for larger ones may be overgrown and tend to be slightly bitter. If you spot a reddish discoloration at stem end, don't be concerned, for this is nature's way of sealing the cut that was made when the head was picked.

• As a general rule, you can count on about 4 servings from a medium-size head of iceberg lettuce, or 1 pound of loose greens, or a 1½-pound head of cabbage.

• For cost-cutting on sandwiches, try baking your own breads, slicing cheeses yourself and buying luncheon meats unsliced.

FRUITS & VEGETABLES: GENERAL BUYING TIPS

• Be alert to price changes in fresh fruits and vegetables. A rule of thumb: Buy seasonal fresh foods when they're most plentiful in your area; the prices will normally be lower then. Also, buy only what you'll use in a short time (with the exceptions of onions and potatoes which will keep). In general, September is the peak of the harvest for many fruits and vegetables that are locally grown. At other times, frozen and canned fruits and vegetables may be your best buys.

• Prices of canned and frozen fruits and vegetables are influenced by seasonal changes just the way fresh fruits and vegetables are. Normally, there will be a substantial—perhaps even dramatic—drop in prices about the time a new crop is packed. During these weeks, which usually occur in late spring or summer, you might see six cans of vegetables on sale.

• If you have any yard space to spare for growing vegetables, you'll be way ahead on savings when winter comes.

• Canned mushrooms cost *more* than fresh ones. Many people think the reverse is true, but the canned variety—even the pieces and stems—are 50 percent more expensive. If you like to cook with mushrooms, buy them fresh in large quantities when on sale, and freeze them.

• Fruits and vegetables that are reduced for quick sale rate consideration if you are buying them for immediate use. Also, don't hesitate to buy fruits that freeze well. Even near-overripe bananas can be frozen. The skin will blacken but the inside will still be fine for use in cakes, breads, etc. Or, you can remove the peel before freezing, blend the fruit with other ingredients and then freeze it.

• When oranges are in season, the cost is usually very reasonable, but it still pays to compare the price of the loose ones to the packaged fruit. (Generally the packaged fruit is less expensive.)

• When buying loose-packed frozen vegetables, it pays to look for the larger sizes. Those packed in clear plastic bags are especially good buys. For one thing, you can see exactly what you're buying. You also have the advantage of using whatever you need at any given time and placing the remainder back in the freezer. Savings of up to 40 percent are often possible.

• The difference between grades of canned fruits and vegetables is not a difference in quality, but of appearance. You do not need to buy fancy grades for stews, soups, pies, etc. Lower grades are just as nutritious, the flavor is often just as good and the price is usually lower. What is different may be the color (as in tomatoes or peas), size and uniformity of pieces (as in peach slices) or tenderness.

SALAD NICOISE

- 5 medium-size potatoes, cooked, drained and cooled
- ½ pound fresh green beans, cooked, drained and cooled
- ⅔ cup vegetable oil
- ⅓ cup wine vinegar
- 2 cloves garlic, crushed
- 1 tablespoon prepared mustard
- 1 tablespoon chopped parsley
- ½ teaspoon instant minced onion
- 1 teaspoon salt
- ¼ teaspoon ground pepper
- 2 large tomatoes, cut into slices
- 1 red onion, cubed
- 1 small green pepper, seeded and cubed
- 6 ripe olives, halved
- 3 hard-cooked eggs, shelled and sliced
- 1 can (2 ounces) anchovy fillets, drained
- 2 medium-size heads of romaine
- 1 can (14 ounces) tuna fish, drained

1. Peel potatoes and cut into thick slices. Place in a shallow dish. Place beans in a second shallow dish.
2. Combine oil, vinegar, garlic, mustard, parsley, onion, salt and pepper in a jar with a tight-fitting lid; shake well to mix. Drizzle ½ cup over potatoes and 2 tablespoonfuls over beans; let each stand at least 30 minutes to season.
3. Layer vegetables, eggs, anchovies and romaine in a large salad bowl. Break tuna into chunks; arrange on top. Pour rest of dressing over; toss lightly in order to blend flavors. Makes 6 servings.

CHICKEN SALAD

- 1 broiler-fryer, weighing about 3 pounds
- 2 cups water
- 1 teaspoon seasoned salt
- ¼ teaspoon seasoned pepper
- 1 large onion, chopped (1 cup)
  Few sprigs of parsley
- 1 can (4 ounces) pimiento, drained and chopped
- 1 small clove of garlic, finely chopped
- ¼ cup vegetable oil
- ¼ cup catsup
- 2 tablespoons vinegar
- 1 tablespoon prepared mustard

- ½ teaspoon salt
- ½ teaspoon leaf rosemary, crumbled
- 1 cup uncooked regular rice
- 1 package (10 ounces) frozen peas, cooked
  Romaine leaves, broken

1. Place chicken in a large kettle or Dutch oven with water to cover, seasoned salt and pepper, ½ cup of the chopped onion and parsley; bring to boiling; reduce heat; cover. Simmer 45 minutes, or until chicken is tender; remove chicken from kettle; cool; strain broth; reserve.
2. Remove meat from bones; cut into bite-size pieces. Place chicken in a large bowl with remaining ½ cup onion, pimiento and garlic.
3. Stir oil, catsup, vinegar, mustard, salt and rosemary in a small bowl until well blended; pour over chicken; toss and cover. Then let stand at room temperature to season, while cooking the rice.
4. Cook rice following label directions, using reserved chicken broth for part of the liquid. Cool.
5. Add cooked peas and rice to chicken; toss lightly. Serve on washed romaine leaves. Makes 6 servings.

STEAK MEDALLIONS

- 3 medium-size onions, peeled and sliced thin
- 2 medium-size green peppers, seeded and sliced into thin rings
- 4 tablespoons (½ stick) butter or margarine
- 4 cube steaks or individual boneless steaks, cut about ¼ inch thick
- 4 hero rolls
- 2 medium-size tomatoes, each cut in 8 slices
- ½ teaspoon seasoned salt
- ½ teaspoon seasoned pepper

1. Sauté onions and green peppers in 2 tablespoons of the butter or margarine until soft in a large frying pan; remove with a slotted spoon and keep warm.
2. Sauté steaks in same frying pan 2 minutes on each side, or until done as you like beef.
3. Split rolls almost through; open out flat. Spread with remaining 2 tablespoons butter or margarine; place on serving plates.
4. Place tomato slices and steaks on rolls; sprinkle with salt and pepper. Spoon onion mixture over steaks. Serve hot with corn chips and a cola beverage, if you wish. Makes 4 servings.

Left: Salad Nicoise, chock-full of hefty chunks of tuna, potatoes, tomatoes, eggs and anchovies, is as satisfying as any meat-and-potatoes meal.

MACARONI AND HAM SALAD

    2 cups uncooked elbow macaroni
    2 cups cooked diced ham (½ pound)
    ½ cup chopped green pepper
    1 small onion, chopped (¼ cup)
    ¾ cup mayonnaise or salad dressing
    ½ teaspoon salt
    ⅛ teaspoon pepper
    1 pint cherry tomatoes, halved

1. Cook macaroni, following label directions; drain well. Cool.
2. Combine macaroni, ham, green pepper and onion in large bowl. Add mayonnaise, salt and pepper; toss to mix. Chill well.
3. Just before serving, halve 1 cup cherry tomatoes; add to salad; toss lightly to mix. Garnish with remaining tomatoes. Makes 8 servings.

SALMON MOUSSE

    2 envelopes unflavored gelatin
    2 cups water
    ¼ cup lemon juice
    1 envelope or teaspoon instant vegetable broth
    1 can (1 pound) salmon
    ¾ cup finely chopped celery
    ½ cup finely chopped seeded red pepper
    2 tablespoons chopped parsley
    2 tablespoons grated onion
    ½ teaspoon salt
    ¾ cup mayonnaise or salad dressing

1. Soften gelatin in 1 cup water in a medium-size saucepan. Heat, stirring constantly, until gelatin dissolves; remove from heat; cool; stir in 2 tablespoons lemon juice. Measure out ¾ cup of mixture and reserve.
2. Stir remaining 1 cup of water and instant vegetable broth into remaining mixture in saucepan. Heat, stirring constantly, just until hot.
3. Drain salmon and flake, removing bones and skin. Combine in medium-size bowl with celery, red pepper, parsley, grated onion, salt and mayonnaise or salad dressing. Stir in the ¾ cup gelatin mixture from Step 1. Reserve while preparing mold.
4. Pour half the remaining gelatin mixture into bottom of a 6-cup fish-shape mold; place in a large pan of ice and water; let stand, turning mold often from side to side, to form a thin coat of gelatin on bottom and sides of mold.
5. Spoon salmon mixture over gelatin-coated mold, spreading to cover mold completely.
6. Chill in refrigerator 4 hours, or until firm.
7. When ready to serve, run a sharp-tip thin-blade knife around top of salad; dip mold very quickly in and out of hot water. Cover with a chilled serving plate; turn upside down; shake gently; lift off mold. Garnish with cucumber slices and red pepper slices, and serve with mayonnaise or salad dressing, if you wish. Makes 6 servings.

CHEF'S SALAD

    1 chicken breast, weighing about 12 ounces
    2 cups water
      Few celery tops
    1 small onion, halved
    1½ teaspoons salt
    ¾ cup chili sauce
    ½ cup mayonnaise or salad dressing
    1 teaspoon instant minced onion
    ½ teaspoon sugar
    6 cups broken mixed salad greens
    1 package (3½ ounces) sliced tongue, rolled in cone shapes
    1 package (8 ounces) sliced cooked ham, cut in thin strips
    1 package (8 ounces) sliced process Swiss cheese, cut in thin strips
    1 large tomato, cut into wedges
    1 small cucumber, pared and thinly sliced
    1 hard-cooked egg, sieved

1. Combine chicken breast, water, celery, onion and 1 teaspoon of the salt in a medium-size saucepan; heat to boiling; cover. Simmer 30 minutes, or until chicken is tender. Remove from broth; cool. Chill about 45 minutes. Skin and bone, then cut chicken in cubes.
2. Blend chili sauce, mayonnaise or salad dressing, instant minced onion, sugar and remaining ½ teaspoon salt in a small bowl. Chill dressing 30 minutes.
3. Place greens in a large salad bowl. Arrange tongue, ham, chicken, Swiss cheese, tomatoes and cucumber slices in sections on top. Sprinkle with sieved egg.
4. Just before serving, spoon on dressing; toss to mix. Makes 6 servings.

HOT TUNA HEROES

- 2 cans (about 7 ounces each) tuna fish
- 1 cup chopped celery
- 1 pound fresh peas, shelled (1 cup)
- 4 slices process Swiss cheese, cubed
- ¼ cup chopped parsley
- ¾ cup mayonnaise or salad dressing
- 6 hero rolls
- 4 tablespoons (½ stick) butter or margarine, melted

1. Drain tuna; separate into small-size chunks. Place in a medium-size bowl.
2. Add celery, peas, cheese and parsley; fold in mayonnaise or salad dressing.
3. Cut a slice from top of each roll; hollow out inside, leaving a ½-inch-thick shell. Brush insides of shells with melted butter or margarine; fill with tuna fish mixture. Wrap each separately in foil.
4. Bake in hot oven (400°) 15 minutes, or just until filling is hot. Thread a lemon wedge and 2 ripe olives onto a wooden pick to serve with each sandwich, if you wish. Serve hot. Makes 6 servings.

CHICKEN SALAD DELUXE

- 1 broiler-fryer (about 3 pounds)
- 4 cups water
- 1 small onion, sliced
- Few celery tops
- ¼ teaspoon salt
- ⅓ cup mayonnaise or salad dressing
- ⅓ cup dairy sour cream
- 1 tablespoon lemon juice
- ¼ teaspoon pepper
- ¾ cup chopped celery
- 1 medium-size onion, chopped (½ cup)
- ¼ cup chopped dill pickle
- Lettuce
- Paprika

1. Combine chicken with water, sliced onion, celery tops and salt in a kettle or Dutch oven. Heat to boiling; reduce heat; cover; simmer about 1 hour, or until chicken is tender. Remove from broth and cool until easy to handle. (Save broth to start a soup another day.)
2. Skin the chicken and take meat from bones.

Cut meat into bite-size pieces; place in a bowl.
3. Blend mayonnaise or salad dressing, sour cream, lemon juice and pepper in a small bowl. Combine celery, onion and dill pickle with chicken; add the dressing; toss until evenly coated. Cover; chill at least an hour to season and blend flavors.
4. Line salad bowl with lettuce leaves. Spoon salad into bowl. Sprinkle with paprika. Makes 4 servings.

BAVARIAN BAKED POTATO SALAD

- 5 medium-size potatoes (about 2 pounds)
- 1 pound frankfurters, cut into 1-inch pieces
- 2 tablespoons vegetable oil
- 1 medium-size onion, chopped (½ cup)
- 2 tablespoons flour
- 3 tablespoons brown sugar
- 1 teaspoon salt
- 1 teaspoon dry mustard
- ⅛ teaspoon pepper
- 1 cup water
- ⅓ cup vinegar
- 1 cup thinly sliced celery
- ½ cup chopped green pepper
- ¼ cup chopped pimiento
- 1 package (8 ounces) process sliced American cheese

1. Cook potatoes in boiling salted water in a large saucepan 30 minutes, or until tender; drain. Cool until easy to handle, then peel and dice. Place in a medium-size bowl.
2. Brown frankfurters in oil in a medium-size skillet; remove with a slotted spoon to the bowl with potatoes.
3. Saute onion in same skillet until soft. Combine flour, sugar, salt, mustard and pepper; stir into drippings; cook, stirring constantly, until bubbly. Stir in water and vinegar; continue cooking and stirring until dressing thickens and bubbles 1 minute.
4. Add celery, green pepper and pimiento; cook 1 minute longer. Pour over potatoes and frankfurters. Spoon one half of the potato mixture into an 8-cup baking dish; layer with 4 slices of cheese; spoon remaining potato mixture into dish. Top with remaining cheese slices cut into triangles.
5. Bake in moderate oven (350°) 15 minutes, or until cheese is melted. Makes 6 servings.

TIJUANA TOASTIES

    6 flat corn-meal cakes (6 to a package)
    1 pound ground beef
    1 small onion, chopped (¼ cup)
    2 tablespoons butter or margarine
    2 teaspoons chili powder
    1 teaspoon salt
    2 cans (1 pound each) barbecue beans
    1 cup shredded iceberg lettuce
    1 package (4 ounces) shredded
       Cheddar cheese

1. Split corn-meal cakes with a sharp knife; place, cut sides up, on a cooky sheet.
2. Shape ground beef into a patty in a large frying pan. Cook 5 minutes on each side, then break up into small chunks; push to one side. Add onion and butter or margarine to pan; sauté 3 minutes, or until onion is soft. Stir in chili powder and salt; cook 1 minute. Stir in beans; heat slowly to boiling.
3. Heat corn cakes in broiler 2 to 3 minutes, or just until toasted; place 2 pieces on each of 6 serving plates. Spoon beef mixture on top. Sprinkle lettuce over half and grated cheese over remainder. Serve hot with corn chips, if you wish. Makes 6 servings.

HEIDELBERGS

    1 can (1 pound, 11 ounces) sauerkraut
    1 tart apple, halved, cored and diced
    3 tablespoons sugar
    1 package (¾ pound) smoked sausage links
    1 tablespoon butter or margarine
    ½ cup mayonnaise or salad dressing
    ½ cup chili sauce
    1 teaspoon instant minced onion
    ½ cup grated Cheddar cheese
    8 large slices caraway rye bread

1. Drain liquid from sauerkraut. Combine sauerkraut with apple and sugar in a medium-size saucepan; heat to boiling; cover. Simmer 15 minutes to blend flavors; drain.
2. Split sausages lengthwise; sauté in butter or margarine until lightly browned in a medium-size frying pan.
3. Blend mayonnaise or salad dressing with chili sauce, onion and cheese in a small bowl.
4. Place 2 slices of bread on each of 4 serving

plates; spread each with part of the mayonnaise mixture. Layer sauerkraut, remaining mayonnaise mixture and sausages on top. Garnish each with a sprig of parsley and serve with sour pickles, if you wish. Makes 4 servings.

GRILLED CHEESE FOR A CROWD

    ½ cup mayonnaise or salad dressing
    ¼ cup finely chopped dill pickle
   24 slices white bread
    3 packages (8 ounces each) sliced provolone
       cheese
    ½ cup (1 stick) butter or margarine, melted

1. Mix mayonnaise or salad dressing and pickle in a small bowl; spread 1 rounded teaspoonful on each slice of bread.
2. Place cheese on half the bread slices, cutting cheese to fit; top with remaining bread, spread side down. Brush sandwiches lightly on both sides with melted butter or margarine; place on cooky sheets.
3. Bake in extremely hot oven (500°) 5 minutes, or until golden and cheese is melted. (No need to turn.) Cut each sandwich in half diagonally; serve immediately on a large serving platter. Makes 12 servings.

RHINELAND POTATO SALAD

    4 large potatoes
    1 pound frankfurters
    3 tablespoons vegetable oil
    1 large onion, chopped (1 cup)
    1 large green pepper, halved, seeded and
       chopped
    1 large red pepper, halved, seeded and
       chopped
    2 teaspoons salt
    ¼ teaspoon ground pepper
    ⅓ cup vinegar

1. Peel potatoes; cut into thin slices. Cook in boiling salted water 15 minutes, or just until tender; drain well.
2. Cut frankfurters into thin slices. Brown in oil in a large skillet; push to one side; add onion; sauté until soft. Add chopped peppers, salt, ground pepper and vinegar; cook, stirring constantly, for about 2 minutes. (To page 115.)

3. Add drained potatoes to skillet; toss gently to mix. Spoon into serving bowl and serve warm. Makes 4 servings.

SPAGHETTI PORKERS

    1 package (8 ounces) heat-and-serve sausages, cut in 1-inch pieces
    2 cans (15 ounces each) spaghetti in tomato sauce
    ¾ teaspoon Italian seasoning
    4 hero rolls, split and buttered
    1 green pepper, seeded and cut in thin rings

1. Brown sausages in a medium-size frying pan; stir in spaghetti and Italian seasoning. Heat slowly, stirring once or twice, until bubbly.
2. Put rolls together with spaghetti filling, dividing evenly; top with green-pepper rings. Offer Parmesan cheese to sprinkle over filling, if you wish. Serve hot. Makes 4 servings.

GERMAN POTATO AND EGG SALAD

    5 medium-size potatoes (about 2 pounds)
    8 hard-cooked eggs, shelled and coarsely chopped
    4 ounces Swiss cheese, cubed (1 cup)
    1 cup cubed ham (or any leftover cold cut you wish)
    2 tablespoons vegetable oil
    1 medium-size onion, chopped (½ cup)
    2 tablespoons flour
    1 tablespoon sugar
    ¾ teaspoon salt
    1 teaspoon dry mustard
    1⅓ cups water
    ⅓ cup vinegar
    ½ cup chopped green pepper
    ¼ cup chopped pimiento

1. Cook potatoes in boiling salted water in a large saucepan 30 minutes, or until tender; drain. Cool until easy to handle, then peel and dice. Place in a 10-cup baking dish; add hard-cooked eggs and Swiss cheese.
2. Brown ham or other leftover meat in oil in a medium-size skillet; remove with a slotted spoon; reserve for Step 4.
3. Sauté onion in same skillet until soft. Combine flour, sugar, salt and dry mustard; stir into drippings. Cook, stirring constantly, until bubbly. Stir in water and vinegar; continue cooking and stirring until dressing thickens and bubbles 1 minute.
4. Add green pepper and pimiento; cook 1 minute longer. Pour over potato and egg mixture; toss lightly until combined; sprinkle with the reserved ham.
5. Serve warm or bake in moderate oven (325°) 10 minutes, or until mixture is piping-hot. Serve from the baking dish or spoon onto individual plates in the kitchen. Makes 8 servings.

PÂTÉ SUPPER SANDWICHES

    ½ pound sliced bacon
    1 pound chicken livers
    2 tablespoons chopped onion
    1 can (3 or 4 ounces) sliced mushrooms
    1¼ teaspoons salt
    2 teaspoons Worcestershire sauce
    4 tablespoons (½ stick) butter or margarine
    3 medium-size tomatoes, sliced thin
    2 teaspoons sugar
    ¼ teaspoon pepper
    ¼ cup chopped parsley
    12 large slices rye bread

1. Sauté bacon until crisp in a medium-size frying pan; remove and drain on paper toweling; keep warm. Pour all drippings from pan, then measure 2 tablespoonfuls and return to pan.
2. Stir chicken livers and onion into pan. Cook slowly, stirring constantly, 5 minutes, or until browned; stir in mushrooms and liquid, ¼ teaspoon of the salt, and Worcestershire sauce. Cook, stirring several times, 5 minutes, or until liquid evaporates. Mash mixture well with a fork.
3. While livers cook, melt butter or margarine in a jelly-roll pan; place tomatoes in a single layer in pan; sprinkle with sugar, remaining 1 teaspoon salt and pepper.
4. Heat in moderate oven (350°) 5 minutes, or just until hot; sprinkle with parsley.
5. Place each of 6 slices of bread on a serving plate; top with tomatoes, then drizzle buttery drippings from pan over tomatoes. Spread liver mixture over tomatoes, dividing evenly. Top with bacon and remaining bread slices. Cut each sandwich in half; serve hot with potato chips and dill pickles, if you wish. Makes 6 servings.

SALADS & SANDWICHES

TUNA MOLD

- 1 package (10 ounces) frozen peas
- 1 can (7 ounces) solid-pack tuna
- 1 small onion, finely chopped (¼ cup)
- ¼ cup diced pimiento
- 1 envelope unflavored gelatin
- ¼ cup cold water
- 2 tablespoons sugar
- ½ teaspoon salt
- ⅛ teaspoon pepper
- ½ cup boiling water
- ¼ cup lemon juice
- ½ cup mayonnaise or salad dressing

1. Cook peas and drain. Drain and flake tuna. Combine peas, tuna, onion and pimiento; toss.
2. Soften gelatin in cold water. Add sugar, salt, pepper and boiling water; stir until gelatin is dissolved. Add lemon juice and mayonnaise or salad dressing; stir until smooth. Chill until syrupy.
3. Spoon tuna mixture into a 4-cup mold. Carefully pour gelatin mixture into mold. Insert a small spatula at intervals through the mixture to allow gelatin to reach the bottom of the mold.
4. Refrigerate until firm, about 3 hours. Unmold as in Salmon Mousse (page 112). Garnish with salad greens, if you wish. Makes 4 servings.

CHICKEN SALAD WITH CAPERS

- 2 chicken breasts (about 12 ounces each), cooked
- ½ cup chopped celery
- 2 tablespoons finely chopped onion
- ⅓ cup mayonnaise or salad dressing
- 1 tablespoon lemon juice
- 2 tablespoons drained capers
- ½ teaspoon salt
- ⅛ teaspoon pepper

1. Remove skin and bones from chicken breasts; cut meat into generous pieces (there should be about 3 cups).
2. Combine chicken, celery and onion in a medium-size bowl. Blend mayonnaise or salad dressing with lemon juice; add to chicken mixture with capers, salt and pepper. Toss well to coat. Chill well. Makes 4 servings.

HAM-AND-CHEESE WAFFLES

- 3 tablespoons prepared mustard
- 3 tablespoons mayonnaise or salad dressing
- 12 slices white sandwich bread
- 6 slices process American cheese (from an 8-ounce package)
- 6 slices spiced ham (from an 8-ounce package)
- 6 tablespoons (¾ stick) butter or margarine

1. Blend mustard and mayonnaise or salad dressing in a cup; spread over bread.
2. Cover each of 6 slices with cheese, then spiced ham; top with remaining bread. Spread outsides of sandwiches with butter or margarine.
3. Bake in preheated waffle iron 4 to 5 minutes, or until golden and cheese melts. Cut in half diagonally; place 3 halves on each serving plate. Serve hot with deviled eggs, bean salad and milk, if you wish. Makes 4 servings.

HAM, CHICKEN AND CHEESE LOAF

- 2 envelopes unflavored gelatin
- ½ cup cold water
- ½ teaspoon salt
- ⅛ teaspoon pepper
- 1 teaspoon grated onion
- 1 tablespoon lemon juice
- 1 cup boiling water
- ½ cup mayonnaise or salad dressing
- 1 cup dairy sour cream
- 1½ ounces Roquefort cheese, crumbled (½ cup)
- 2 cups diced cooked ham
- 2 cups diced cooked chicken
- 1 cup finely chopped celery

1. Soften gelatin in cold water. Add salt, pepper, onion, lemon juice and boiling water; stir until gelatin is dissolved. Add mayonnaise or salad dressing, sour cream and cheese; stir until smooth. Chill over ice and water, stirring constantly, until as thick as unbeaten egg white.
2. Fold in ham, chicken and celery. Turn into a 9x5x3-inch loaf pan.
3. Refrigerate until firm, about 3 hours. Unmold as in Salmon Mousse (page 112). Garnish with salad greens and radish roses, if you wish. Makes 8 to 10 servings.

11
MAKE LEFTOVERS COUNT

Everyone has leftovers. But not everyone knows what to do with them. As a result, they often end up in the garbage—and you end up spending more than you need to every week of the year. This chapter is devoted to showing you what to do with some of the most common types of leftover meats. We've also included several recipes that start with a roast and follow-up with a recipe for an equally delicious second meal. In other sections of the book, such as in the soup and casserole chapters, you'll find additional ideas for using leftovers effectively. All are geared to not only helping you get more for your money, but to making leftovers taste and look just as good as when you served the same foods the first time around.

LEFTOVERS

BOEUF A LA MODE EN GELEE

- 3 **medium carrots, pared and cut in ½-inch slices**
- 1 **pint Brussels sprouts, washed and trimmed**
- 2 **cans condensed beef broth**
- 1⅓ **cups water**
- 2 **envelopes unflavored gelatin**
- 3 **tablespoons Madeira or dry sherry**
- 6 **drops liquid red-pepper seasoning**
- 1 **pound cooked roast beef or steak, sliced thin**
  Watercress
  Horseradish Dressing (recipe follows)

1. Cook carrots and Brussels sprouts separately in boiling salted water, 15 minutes or until tender. Drain; chill.
2. Combine beef broth and water in medium-size bowl. Soften gelatin in 1 cup of broth, about 5 minutes, in a small saucepan. Heat, stirring constantly, until gelatin dissolves; stir into remaining broth in bowl. Add Madeira and red-pepper seasoning. Cut Brussels sprouts in half lengthwise.
3. Pour ¾ cup of the gelatin mixture into an 11x7x1½-inch pan or an 8-cup shallow mold; place in a larger pan of ice and water until gelatin is sticky-firm. Arrange part of the Brussels sprouts and carrots in decorative pattern along sides of pan. Make 12 rolls or bundles of meat slices; place 6 down center of pan, spacing evenly; spoon several tablespoons of remaining gelatin mixture over vegetables and meat. Arrange some of remaining Brussels sprouts against sides of pan. Add enough gelatin mixture to almost cover meat. Chill until sticky-firm.
4. Arrange remaining meat and vegetables on top of first layer in pan; set pan on shelf in refrigerator; carefully spoon remaining gelatin over to cover meat and vegetables completely. Chill until firm, several hours or overnight.
5. Just before serving, loosen gelatin around edges with a knife; dip pan quickly in and out of hot water; wipe off water. Cover pan with serving plate; turn upside down; shake gently; lift off mold. Border with watercress, if you wish. Serve with Horseradish Dressing. Makes 6 servings.
HORSERADISH DRESSING—Combine ¾ cup mayonnaise or salad dressing; 1 hard-cooked egg, sieved; 1 tablespoon tarragon vinegar; and 1 teaspoon prepared horseradish in a small bowl; stir to blend well. Cover; refrigerate to blend flavors. Makes 1 cup.

CORNISH BEEF HASH AND EGG PIE

- 3 **medium-size onions, chopped (1½ cups)**
- 2 **tablespoons butter or margarine**
- 2½ **cups chopped cooked corned beef (¾ pound)**
- 3 **cups chopped boiled potatoes**
- 1 **teaspoon Worcestershire sauce**
- ½ **teaspoon salt**
- ¼ **teaspoon pepper**
- 1 **package piecrust mix**
- ¼ **cup milk**
- 6 **eggs**

1. Sauté onion in butter or margarine until soft in medium-size skillet, about 5 minutes.
2. Combine corned beef, potatoes, onions, Worcestershire sauce, salt and pepper in a large bowl; toss to mix well with a fork.
3. Prepare piecrust mix, following label directions or make pastry from your favorite two-crust recipe. Roll out ½ of pastry to a 12-inch round on a lightly floured board; fit into a 9-inch, deep pie plate. Trim any crust overhang to ½ inch.
4. Spoon hash mixture into prepared pastry shell, mounding center higher than sides. Scoop a hollow about 1½ inches wide, 1 inch in from edge all around. Drizzle milk over hash. Break eggs into hollow, spacing evenly.
5. Roll out remaining pastry to an 11-inch round; cut several slits near center to let steam escape; cover pie. Trim overhang to ½ inch; turn edge under, flush with rim; flute edge. Roll out trimmings to make fancy cutouts for top, if you wish. Brush top and cutouts with milk.
6. Bake in very hot oven (450°) for 10 minutes, reduce heat to 400° and bake 15 minutes longer, or until pastry is golden. Cut into wedges and serve hot. Makes 6 servings.

HAM AND LIMA CASSEROLE

- 2 **tablespoons butter or margarine**
- 1 **small onion, chopped (¼ cup)**
- 1 **can (1 pound) tomatoes**
- ½ **teaspoon salt**

Three great dinners, each offering a way to plan for leftovers, are shown at right. From top to bottom: Boned Capon Roast, Roast Lamb, Middle-Eastern Style, and Potted Pork Roast. On page 120, the leftovers: Souffléed Chicken Supreme, Moussaka à la Turque, and Oriental Pork Platter.

⅛ teaspoon pepper
2 package (10 ounces each) frozen baby lima beans, cooked and drained
2 cups cubed, cooked ham
1 tablespoon butter or margarine, melted
¼ cup packaged bread crumbs

1. Melt the 2 tablespoons butter or margarine in large skillet; sauté onion until tender. Stir in tomatoes, salt and pepper.
2. Arrange limas and ham in layers in a shallow 8-cup baking dish. Pour tomato mixture over limas and ham. Combine the 1 tablespoon melted butter and bread crumbs in a small bowl; sprinkle over top of casserole.
3. Bake in a moderate oven (375°) 30 minutes, or until sauce is bubbly. Makes 6 servings.

SWEET AND PUNGENT PORK

3½ cups cooked pork (1¼ pounds), cut into ¾-inch cubes
1 tablespoon soy sauce
1 egg, slightly beaten
Oil for frying
½ cup cornstarch (for coating)
Sauce:
1 large onion, chopped (1 cup)
1 large green pepper, halved, seeded and cut into strips
3 carrots, pared and sliced very thin, (about 1 cup)
1 tablespoon vegetable oil
1 tablespoon cornstarch
1 cup water
5 tablespoons vinegar
¼ cup firmly packed light brown sugar
1 envelope or teaspoon instant chicken broth
1 can (about 13 ounces) pineapple tidbits

1. Combine pork with soy sauce in a medium-size bowl; toss to mix with fork; cover. Let stand at room temperature 30 minutes. Add egg, toss to coat meat well with egg.
2. Pour enough vegetable oil to make 1-inch depth in a medium-size skillet or saucepan; heat to 375° on deep-fat thermometer.
3. Place ½ cup cornstarch in a plastic bag; add pork cubes and shake bag until meat is well coated with cornstarch.
4. Sauté pork, about a third at a time, in the hot oil 3 minutes, or until golden brown and

coating is crisp. Lift out with a slotted spoon; drain on paper toweling. Keep warm.
5. Sauté onion, green pepper and carrots in oil in large skillet 2 to 3 minutes, or until vegetables are crisply tender.
6. Mix 1 tablespoon cornstarch with 2 tablespoons water in cup. Add remaining water, vinegar, sugar and chicken broth to skillet; bring to boiling; cover; reduce heat; simmer 5 minutes. Stir in pineapple and cornstarch mixture; bring to boiling, stirring constantly; cover; cook just until thickened, about 1 minute.
7. Just before serving, combine the sweet-and-pungent sauce with pork. Then serve with hot cooked rice and additional soy sauce, if you desire. Makes 6 servings.

HAM AND POTATOES AU GRATIN

2 tablespoons butter or margarine
1 small onion, chopped (¼ cup)
2 tablespoons flour
1¾ cups milk
½ teaspoon salt
⅛ teaspoon pepper
1½ pounds potatoes, pared and diced, (about 3 cups)
4 wedges Gruyère cheese (from a 6-ounce package), shredded
6 slices cooked ham (about ¼-inch thick)

1. Melt butter in saucepan; sauté onion until tender. Stir in flour; cook until bubbly. Add milk. Cook over medium heat, stirring constantly, until sauce thickens. Add salt and pepper.
2. Layer diced potatoes and cheese in a buttered, deep, 6-cup baking dish. Pour over sauce; mix lightly. Cover.
3. Bake in a moderate oven (350°) 1 hour, or until potatoes are tender. Uncover; top with ham slices; cover. Bake 15 minutes longer. Makes 6 servings.

ADRIATIC LAMB PIE

2 hot Italian sausages (6 ounces)
3 small yellow onions, peeled and quartered
1 small green pepper, halved, seeded and diced (½ cup)
2½ cups cooked cubed lamb

2 tablespoons vegetable oil
1 small eggplant, pared and cubed (3 cups)
3 tablespoons flour
1 can (1 pound) tomatoes
2 cups water
1 envelope or teaspoon instant beef broth
1 teaspoon salt
½ teaspoon leaf basil, crumbled
½ teaspoon leaf rosemary, crumbled
2 zucchini, washed, trimmed and sliced
1 package (8 ounces) refrigerated buttermilk biscuits

1. Slice sausages into 1-inch pieces; brown in large skillet. Add onions and pepper, sauté until soft in drippings from sausage. Remove sausage and vegetables with slotted spoon to a 12-cup baking dish.
2. Brown lamb in same skillet. Remove to baking dish. Add oil and eggplant to skillet; sauté 5 minutes; sprinkle with flour. Stir in tomatoes, water, beef broth, salt, basil and rosemary. Bring to boiling, stirring constantly. Boil 1 minute. Pour over meat in baking dish; add zucchini. Mix well.
3. Roll buttermilk biscuits on a lightly floured pastry board into pencil-thin strips. Arrange on top of stew in a lattice pattern.
4. Bake in moderate oven (375°) 40 minutes, or until pastry is golden brown and pie is bubbly-hot. Makes 6 servings.

DEVILED BEEF SLICES

8 slices cooked beef (¼-inch thick)
2 tablespoons prepared mustard
1 egg
½ teaspoon salt
Few drops red-pepper seasoning
2 tablespoons water
1 cup seasoned fine dry bread crumbs
4 tablespoons vegetable oil

1. Spread beef slices with the prepared mustard.
2. Beat egg in a pie plate. Stir in salt, red-pepper seasoning and water. Sprinkle bread crumbs on wax paper.
3. Dip beef slices first into seasoned egg and then into bread crumbs.
4. Heat oil in a large skillet. Brown beef slices on one side; turn and brown on second side. Serve on a heated platter. Makes 4 servings.

SAVORY STUFFED CABBAGE

1 pound cooked lamb, ground
2 cups cooked rice
1 egg
1 clove garlic, crushed
1 teaspoon salt
¼ teaspoon leaf thyme, crumbled
¼ teaspoon leaf rosemary, crumbled
⅛ teaspoon pepper
1 can (15 ounces) special tomato sauce
1 head of cabbage (about 3½ pounds)
2 tablespoons butter or margarine
1 large onion, chopped (1 cup)
2 teaspoons sugar
½ teaspoon salt
½ cup water

1. Combine lamb, rice, egg, garlic, salt, thyme, rosemary, pepper and ⅔ cup of the tomato sauce in large bowl; mix well with fork.
2. Trim outside leaves from cabbage. Cut a small slice about 3 inches in diameter from top end; set aside. With a sharp-tip knife and hands, hollow out cabbage leaving a shell about ½ inch thick. (Chop cut-out pieces coarsely and cook separately to serve along with stuffed cabbage or save to cook as a vegetable for another day.)
3. Spoon lamb mixture into shell, pressing it down firmly, fit top back into place; tie with a string.
4. Sauté onion in hot butter or margarine in medium-size frying pan until soft, about 5 minutes; add remaining tomato sauce, sugar, salt and water. Bring to boiling, stirring constantly. Remove from heat.
5. Place cabbage, core end down, in a deep flameproof casserole or Dutch oven; pour sauce over; cover. (If cabbage is too high, use an inverted bowl or foil to cover.)
6. Bake in moderate oven (350°), basting 2 or 3 times with sauce, for 1 hour and 30 minutes.
7. Place stuffed cabbage on a heated serving platter; remove string. Spoon some of sauce over cabbage; pass remaining sauce in a separate bowl. Cut cabbage into wedges for serving. Garnish with parsley, if you wish.
SERVING IDEA—Save several of the pretty large outer cabbage leaves. Blanch them in boiling salted water, just before cabbage is served, then wrap leaves around cabbage before serving. Makes 6 servings.

BONED ROAST CAPON

½ pound cooked ham
3 tablespoons dry sherry
1 tablespoon finely chopped shallots or green onion
1 capon, turkey or chicken (about 6 pounds)
2 cups water
   Giblets
½ teaspoon salt
1 pound ground veal
3 eggs
9 tablespoons milk
¼ cup coarsely chopped pistachio nuts
3 tablespoons chopped parsley
1 teaspoon salt
¼ teaspoon pepper
¼ teaspoon leaf thyme, crumbled
   Dash of ground allspice
   Olive Gravy (recipe follows)

1. Cut ham into ½-inch-thick strips; place in a small bowl with sherry and shallots to marinate for about 1 hour.
2. Place capon, breast side down, on cutting board. With a sharp, thin-bladed knife, cut alongside backbone through skin and flesh to the bone. Then, following rib cage with the tip of the knife, cut meat from back and breast bones on both sides, leaving wings and thigh and leg bones intact. Lift out rib cage.
3. Break the rib bones into smaller pieces; place in roasting pan. Roast in hot oven (450°) 20 minutes, or until richly browned. Drain off fat; place bones in a large saucepan with water, neck, gizzard and heart and the ½ teaspoon salt. Cover; simmer about 1 hour. Remove and discard bones; chop gizzard and heart; reserve broth.
4. Combine ⅓ of ground veal, liver from capon, 1 egg and 3 tablespoons of the milk in container of electric blender. Whirl at high speed, just until smooth; turn out into a large bowl. Repeat twice with remaining veal, egg and milk. Stir nuts, parsley, remaining salt, pepper, thyme and allspice into meat mixture.
5. Spread capon, skin side down, on cutting board. Using a darning needle and cotton string, make a few stitches, starting at leg end, to sew skin back together for about 2 inches. Sprinkle with 1 tablespoon of the sherry marinade from Step 1. Arrange a few strips of ham on the capon; spread ⅓ of veal mixture down the center;

arrange ⅓ of remaining ham on top; repeat twice.
6. Continue sewing together until filling is completely enclosed, bringing neck skin down the back to reshape capon as close to original as possible. Tie with string in several places; tie legs together. Place, breast side up, in a small roasting pan; fold a piece of foil and place loosely, as a tent, over bird.
7. Insert meat thermometer into center of filling. Roast in moderate oven (350°), basting often with pan drippings, 2 hours and 25 minutes, or until meat thermometer registers 160°. After about 1½ hours, remove foil to let bird brown nicely. Transfer to a heated platter and keep warm while making gravy. Makes 6 servings plus leftovers.
OLIVE GRAVY—Add reserved broth to roasting pan; bring to boiling over medium heat, scraping off browned bits; strain into a 2-cup measure. Measure 3 tablespoons fat into a small saucepan. Discard rest of fat. Stir 3 tablespoons flour into fat in saucepan; stir over medium heat until flour turns light brown. Blend in drippings (about 1½ cups) and 2 tablespoons Madeira. Cook, stirring constantly, until mixture thickens and bubbles, 3 minutes. Parboil 1 cup stuffed green olives in water to cover for 5 minutes; drain. Add to gravy, along with reserved chopped gizzard and heart. Makes about 2 cups.
Leftover Specialty: Souffléed Chicken Supreme (recipe follows).

SOUFFLÉED CHICKEN SUPREME

1 can condensed cream of shrimp soup
1 cup milk
2 cups cut-up cooked chicken (see Boned Roast Capon)
3 tablespoons butter or margarine
¼ cup flour
¾ cup milk
4 eggs, separated
1 teaspoon salt
   Few drops red-pepper seasoning
¼ teaspoon cream of tartar

1. Blend soup with 1 cup milk. Combine with chicken in 8-cup shallow baking dish.
2. Melt butter or margarine in small saucepan. Blend in flour; cook, stirring constantly, until bubbly. Stir in ¾ cup milk; continue cooking

and stirring until mixture thickens and bubbles 1 minute; cool.

3. Beat yolks with salt and pepper seasoning in a large bowl. Beat in hot mixture.

4. Beat whites with cream of tartar just until stiff peaks form. Fold whites, ½ at a time, into yolk mixture just until well combined. Spoon soufflé mixture over chicken in baking dish.

5. Bake in moderate oven (375°) 40 minutes, or until puffed and browned. Makes 6 servings.

ROAST LAMB, MIDDLE-EASTERN STYLE

1 five-pound leg of lamb
1 bunch green onions
1 large lemon
1 small bunch fresh mint
1½ teaspoons salt
¼ teaspoon freshly ground pepper
3 cups boiling water
4 tablespoons flour

1. Trim all but a thin layer of fat from lamb. Place lamb, trimmed side up, on rack in shallow roasting pan.

2. Chop onions, whole lemon and mint leaves until very fine; blend with 1 teaspoon of the salt and pepper.

3. Press all but ¼ cup of mixture onto surface of lamb. Place roasting pan on rack in oven; pour 3 cups boiling water into pan.

4. Roast in hot oven (425°) 15 minutes; reduce heat to slow (325°) and roast 1 hour and 45 minutes, basting several times with water in pan, for rare lamb. Roast 30 minutes longer for medium lamb. Remove roast from pan to heated serving platter and sprinkle with reserved green onion mixture. Keep in warm place while making gravy.

5. Strain liquid in roasting pan into 4-cup measure; allow to stand 5 minutes; skim off all fat. Return liquid to roasting pan; heat to boiling. Combine flour with ½ cup cold water to make a smooth paste; stir into bubbling liquid. Cook, stirring constantly, until mixture thickens and bubbles 3 minutes. Season with remaining ½ teaspoon salt and serve in heated gravy boat.

6. Garnish platter with lemon wedges and green onions, if you wish. Makes 6 servings plus leftovers.

Leftover Specialty: Moussaka a La Turque (recipe is in the next column; it serves 6).

MOUSSAKA A LA TURQUE

2 large eggplant (about 1¼ pounds each)
2 large onions, chopped (2 cups)
1 clove garlic, minced
4 tablespoons olive or vegetable oil
½ pound fresh mushrooms, chopped
2 cups cooked lamb (see Roast Lamb, Middle-Eastern Style)
3 teaspoons salt
¼ teaspoon pepper
1 teaspoon leaf oregano, crumbled
3 eggs
2 cups soft white bread crumbs (4 slices)

1. Halve eggplant lengthwise; place, cut side down, in a 15x10x1-inch baking pan. Place baking pan on rack in oven; pour boiling water in pan to a depth of one-half inch.

2. Bake in moderate oven (375°) 30 minutes, or until eggplant is soft when pressed with fingertip. Remove eggplant from baking pan; drain on paper toweling.

3. Scoop out inside of eggplant, being careful not to break the skin. (A grapefruit knife does this very easily.) Chop eggplant into small pieces.

4. Sauté onion and garlic in oil until soft in a large skillet; add mushrooms; sauté 3 minutes. Add eggplant and sauté until liquid in pan has evaporated. (Both the mushrooms and eggplant give off liquid when cooked.) Stir in lamb, salt, pepper and oregano; cook 3 minutes; remove from heat.

5. Beat eggs in a large bowl; stir in bread crumbs, then eggplant mixture, until well-blended.

6. Line an 8-cup charlotte mold or straight-sided mold or bowl with eggplant shells, skin side out; spoon eggplant mixture into shells; fold shells over mixture. Cover mold with a double thickness of foil.

7. Place mold on a rack or trivet in a kettle or steamer; pour in boiling water to half the depth of the mold.

8. Bake in moderate oven (375°) 1 hour and 30 minutes; remove mold from water and remove foil cover; allow to stand on wire rack 10 minutes.

9. Unmold onto heated serving platter; remove any excess moisture from platter. Garnish with chopped parsley and a tomato rose, if you wish. Serve immediately. Makes 6 servings.

POTTED PORK ROAST

    1 seven-pound loin of pork
    3 cups dry red wine
    1 large onion, chopped (1 cup)
    6 whole cloves
    6 whole allspice
    1 three-inch piece stick cinnamon
    ½ cup light corn syrup
    4 tablespoons flour
    ½ teaspoon salt
      Duchess Potatoes (recipe follows)
      Buttered carrots
      Buttered zucchini

1. Trim excess fat from pork; place in a glass or plastic container (not aluminum) large enough to hold roast.
2. Heat 1 cup of the wine, onion, cloves, allspice and cinnamon to boiling in a small saucepan. Lower heat; simmer 5 minutes. Combine with remaining wine; pour over pork.
3. Cover container. Refrigerate pork overnight, turning several times in the marinade.
4. Place pork on rack in a shallow roasting pan; score remaining fat in a diamond pattern. Pour marinade over pork.
5. Roast in slow oven (325°), basting often with marinade, 3 hours and 20 minutes, or until a meat thermometer inserted into meat registers almost 170°.
6. Brush roast with corn syrup; roast 10 minutes longer, or until roast is glazed and meat thermometer reads 170°. Place roast on heated platter and keep warm while making sauce.
7. Strain liquid from roasting pan into a 4-cup measure; allow to stand 5 minutes; skim off all fat. Return liquid to pan and heat to bubbling. Combine flour with 1 cup cold water to make a smooth mixture; pour into bubbling liquid in roasting pan.
8. Cook, stirring constantly, until mixture bubbles 3 minutes. Taste; season with salt, if necessary. Pour into heated gravy boat.
9. Serve roast with Duchess Potatoes, buttered carrots and buttered zucchini. Garnish with orange slices and watercress, if you wish. Makes 6 servings plus leftovers.
DUCHESS POTATOES—Pare 2 pounds potatoes; cut into small pieces. Cook in boiling, salted water until tender, about 20 minutes. Mash potatoes; beat in 3 tablespoons butter or margarine, ½ teaspoon salt and 2 beaten eggs. Press out through pastry bag into 6 mounds on buttered cooky sheet. Bake in hot oven (425°) for 15 minutes, or until lightly golden. Makes 6 servings. Leftover Specialty: Oriental Pork Platter (recipe follows).

ORIENTAL PORK PLATTER

    12 thin slices cooked pork (see Potted Pork Roast)
    ½ cup dry sherry
    ¼ cup soy sauce
    3 tablespoons peanut or vegetable oil
    2 medium-size onions, sliced
    2 medium-size green peppers, halved, seeded and cut into cubes
    2 yellow squash, sliced
    ½ pound fresh mushrooms, sliced
      OR: 1 can (6 ounces) sliced mushrooms
    1½ cups water
    1 envelope or teaspoon instant chicken broth
    2 teaspoons salt
    1 can (8 ounces) water chestnuts, drained and sliced
    1 can (4 ounces) pimiento, drained, chopped
    2 tablespoons cornstarch
    ¼ cup cold water
      Hot cooked rice

1. Place pork slices in a shallow pan; combine sherry and soy sauce and pour over meat. Allow to marinate 30 minutes.
2. Heat oil in a large skillet; brown pork quickly in oil; remove from skillet and keep warm.
3. Sauté onion in same skillet just until soft; add green pepper and yellow squash; sauté 2 minutes; add mushrooms and sauté 2 minutes. Add marinade from pork, 1½ cups water, chicken broth and salt.
4. Heat to boiling; cover skillet; lower heat; simmer 5 minutes, or just until vegetables are crisply tender. Add the water chestnuts and the pimiento.
5. Combine cornstarch and cold water to make a smooth paste. Stir into bubbling liquid in skillet. Cook, stirring constantly, 1 minute. Return pork slices; heat 1 minute, or just until thoroughly hot.
6. Line a heated serving platter with hot cooked rice and spoon vegetable mixture over, reserving some of the sauce; arrange pork slices over vegetables; spoon sauce over. Makes 4 servings.

INDEX

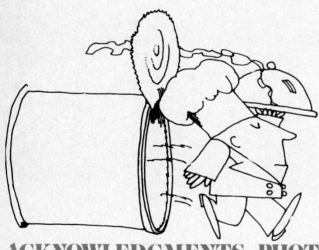

ACKNOWLEDGMENTS, PHOTOGRAPHS & ILLUSTRATIONS

The editor gratefully acknowledges the help of: American Dairy Association; American Egg Board; American Frozen Food Institute; American Gas Association; American Meat Institute; Bazaar de la Cuisine, New York, N.Y.; Virginia H. Knauer, Special Assistant to the President for Consumer Affairs; National Broiler Council; National Fisheries Institute; National Marine Fisheries Service, U.S. Department of Commerce; National Meat & Livestock Institute; The Quaker Oats Company; The Rice Council; U.S. Department of Agriculture; and The Whirlpool Corporation.

All photographs by George Nordhausen except the following:
Alfred Fisher, page 110.
Mort Mace, page 74.
Rudy Muller, pages 22, 102-103.
Gordon Smith, pages 9, 10, 62.
Philip Sykes, pages 4, 12, 15, 33, 45, 71, 83, 101, 109.

Illustrations by:
Adolph Brotman, pages 18-19, 39, 49.
Oni, 5, 13, 31, 43, 53, 65, 81, 91, 97, 107, 117, 128.